PART ONE | LIFE IN OUR AREA

8 CHAPTER ONE
The soldiers

- 8 South Highfields enlists
- 12 Conscientious objectors
- 12 Prisoners of war
- 14 Honouring the dead

15 CHAPTER TWO
Life in South Highfields during the War

- 15 Portrait of a street: Saxe Coburg Street
- 20 Portrait of a street: Laurel Road
- 26 Food
- 29 Children's lives
- 34 Health

39 CHAPTER THREE
Why the street names were changed

- 40 Interning the enemy
- 43 Music
- 43 Patriotism and the press
- 46 Street names

PART TWO | GLOBAL IMPACT AND PEOPLE'S JOURNEYS

52 CHAPTER FOUR
The war in Europe

- 54 Ireland
- 56 Poland
- 60 Turkey
- 61 Serbia
- 62 Czechoslovakia
- 65 Russia
- 67 Germany

72 CHAPTER FIVE
The wider world

- 72 India
- 74 Kurdistan
- 75 Algeria
- 77 Rwanda
- 79 Trinidad and Tobago

83 FINAL WORD

84 FOOTNOTES

86 APPENDIX

- 86 Soldiers
- 87 References for images and recordings

Thank You

This book has been researched and written by a team of local volunteers, most of whom live in South Highfields. Huge thanks to Patrick Breen, Hilary Browne, Javid Bux, Alison Cottam, David Edwards, Alan Fox, Piotr Kuhivchak, Kate Moore, Malcolm Noble, Chris Powis, Kate Sullivan, Andrew Thirlby and Penny Walker.

The people who so generously shared their family stories were Patrick and Piotr above, and Mehmet Aydin, Jean Hill, Jozef Jundzill, Alexander Kazmierz, Alice Klaus, Felicity Kuhivchak, Mustapha Khodjet-Kesba, Werner Menski, Eric Nkundumubano, Ilija Preocanin, Surinderpal Singh Rai and Angela Walker. Thanks to Gillian Lighton for her mother's written memories.

Special thanks to Colin Hyde from the East Midlands Oral History Unit, Dipak Mistry for his photography, Cynthia Brown for her advice on local history and Panikos Paniya for his advice on anti-German issues and John Martin for his advice on food and agriculture. Other advisers include Richard Rodger and Adam Goodwin. Thanks also to Roy Birch, John Chapman, Eileen Gumley, David Humberstone, Catriona Noble, Rowan Roenisch and John Sutton.

We are also grateful for help from Kirby and West Ltd, Leicestershire and Rutland Family History Society, the Friends of Welford Road Cemetery, Leicester Arts and Museums Service and the Records Office for Leicestershire, Leicester and Rutland.

And finally, thanks to our funders the Heritage Lottery Fund and Leicestershire Archaeological and Historical Society.

Introduction

This book offers a unique insight into life in South Highfields, Leicester, during the First World War. It is both local and global in its scope. People who now live in our area have shared their family memories of life in other countries during the War, and we have been privileged to hear some fascinating stories.

Our research has included written and spoken accounts. We have drawn on Council minutes, newspapers, census returns, street directories, burial records and military records. Some of this has involved long days in the Record Office at Wigston, but much more is now available on line through family and military history websites. Inevitably, there are gaps in the story. For example, anyone not staying in their house on the night of the census was not recorded, and some military records from the First World War were destroyed in the Second World War. The full picture will always escape us.

Spoken accounts reveal the real people behind those records, and we are grateful to the East Midland Oral History Archive for preserving them. They are mainly taken from interviews recorded in the 1980s when people were remembering their distant childhoods, usually in working-class families. Most of the accounts we have used were provided by people who lived in South Highfields and the surrounding area at the time. A few are from other parts of Leicester. All are helpful to our story.

South Highfields is the area covered by South Highfields Neighbours, the local residents' association. It extends from the railway station to Evington Road, and from London Road to Sparkenhoe Street and St. Peter's Road. A hundred years ago it was quite a wealthy area with a mix of large houses, substantial terraces and more modest terraces. Most of the houses are still here today, but the larger ones have mainly been converted into small flats and hostels.

There are two parts to this book. The first part, Life in Our Area, is made up of three chapters. Chapter one looks at the soldiers who fought in the War and their families. The second chapter describes daily life during the War years, focusing on two contrasting streets: Saxe Coburg (now Saxby) Street in the wealthier area near the station, and Laurel Road from the other, more working-class area. The third chapter explores anti-German legislation and attitudes, and how our street names came to be changed. The second part of the book, Global Impact and People's Journeys, looks at the wider world and how it was affected by the War. We interviewed people who live here now, or have a strong connection to this area. Their willingness to share their personal stories helps us learn not only about history and politics but also about migration, humanity and inhumanity as it charts their journeys across continents and down through the generations.

There is a great deal of ongoing research into World War One, which will continue to deepen our understanding of that terrible conflict and its impact on the world. This book is one small step in that journey. Those of us from the local residents' association who have compiled it have found it an enriching experience. We think South Highfields is a special place, and invite you, through this book, to learn more about its history, its people and their remarkable stories.

PART ONE | LIFE IN OUR AREA

CHAPTER ONE | The Soldiers

"Stand up the children whose fathers have been killed in the war."

The outbreak of the war saw an initial surge of men signing up to serve in the military. However, this enthusiasm did not last long, and Leicester, in particular, had fewer volunteers than many other towns and cities. By March 1915 just 2.6 per cent of the available population had volunteered, compared to 18 per cent in nearby Nottingham[1]. There may be several reasons for this. There was a strong socialist movement which was largely opposed to the War, and many in non-conformist churches, especially Quakers, Christadelphians and members of the Church of Christ, refused to fight. In towns with high unemployment many more men enlisted, but in Leicester very few people were out of work. Hosiery, together with boot and shoe manufacture were Leicester's main industries, as well as engineering. They were all fulfilling large military orders soon after the war began and employment in these sectors was very high. N.Corah and Sons, for example, made 10 million items of hosiery alone over the period of the war, as well as vests, scarves and cotton helmets. 70 per cent of their goods went to the military. By the end of December 1914 there were no footwear employees out of work. Most companies were making men's boots for the first time, rather than women's and children's boots and shoes. Many engineering factories in Leicester made munitions.

SOUTH HIGHFIELDS ENLISTS

Many First World War military records were lost during the Second World War, but there are records of 128 men from South Highfields serving at some time in the military between 1914 and 1918. Of those, three were already in the army before the War started and one was in the navy. Only 11 joined up in 1914 and a further eight by the end of August 1915. Conscription was introduced in 1916, but late in 1915 the Derby scheme encouraged all eligible men to register for service with the promise that they would only be called up if needed. There was a lot of pressure to get people to volunteer. *"If you don't join voluntarily now, you'll be fetched in a month or two."*[2] Some of those who registered later in the War would have done so because they were too young to register earlier. In Britain, about 250,000 men in the military were under age[3]. For example, Fred Smith of Avon Street was under age when he enlisted, and was discharged the following month. Harry Moulden of Sutherland Street, on the other hand, signed up at the age of 51. The appendix has a street-by-street list of South Highfields men who served in the military during 1914-18.

(Record Office)

The Soldiers

More than a quarter of young men who tried to enlist were found to be unfit for the army or too small[4]. These restrictions were lessened as the war went on. Many men who did make it to the front lines and were later injured were often nursed back to health, only to return to battle. The war had a huge impact in the home. About half as many men were left disabled as were killed in the war, and many soldiers suffered physical and mental health problems for the rest of their lives. This must have been devastating for them and their families.

When the War started, many expected it to be over by Christmas, but it soon became obvious that no end was in sight. Truth was hidden by propaganda, limited reporting and a general lack of knowledge of the real horrors of the front. However, the ever-increasing number of deaths listed in the newspapers told its own story, and would have caused much anxiety. The postcards the soldiers were allowed to send were heavily censored, but would have been keenly read and cherished by their family.

This postcard (a view of Rouen, France) was written on 8th August 1916 by Gunner J. W. Gill, 9th Division Royal Field Artillery, and sent to his mother Mary Robinson, living at 81 Skipworth Street. Like all mail home it bears a stamp showing it had been checked and passed by the censor. That week, his unit was "resting" in billets at Calonne Ricouart, a small brick-built mining town about six miles from Béthune.

We don't know what happened next (most of his service records are missing), but one record, for his "Silver War Badge", shows that he was discharged due to wounds in December 1917. It is unknown when or how he was wounded, but this seems likely to have been in October 1917 in the area around Ypres, when the 50th Brigade suffered 168 casualties (including 64 men who had been gassed) out of 725 officers and men. The Brigade war diary only hints at the appalling conditions, merely noting "The weather conditions and the state of the ground hampered the attack, which was only partially successful." This was the first battle of Passchendaele.

John William Gill had a younger brother, Driver George Harold Gill, who enlisted in December 1915 and who also served in the Royal Field Artillery. He was posted to France in mid-December in the following year and joined the 35th Division Ammunition Column in January 1917. He survived the war uninjured, and was finally discharged in February 1920 after serving in the British Army of Occupation, having, coincidentally, been posted to C Battery 50th Brigade, the same Brigade in which his brother previously served.

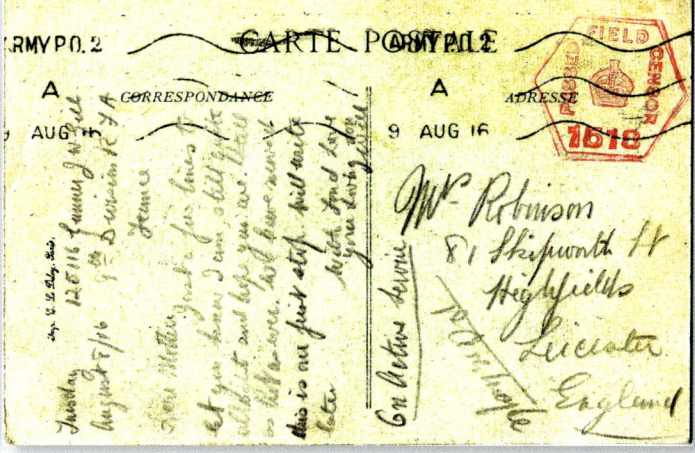

Postcard to 81 Skipworth Street

The Soldiers

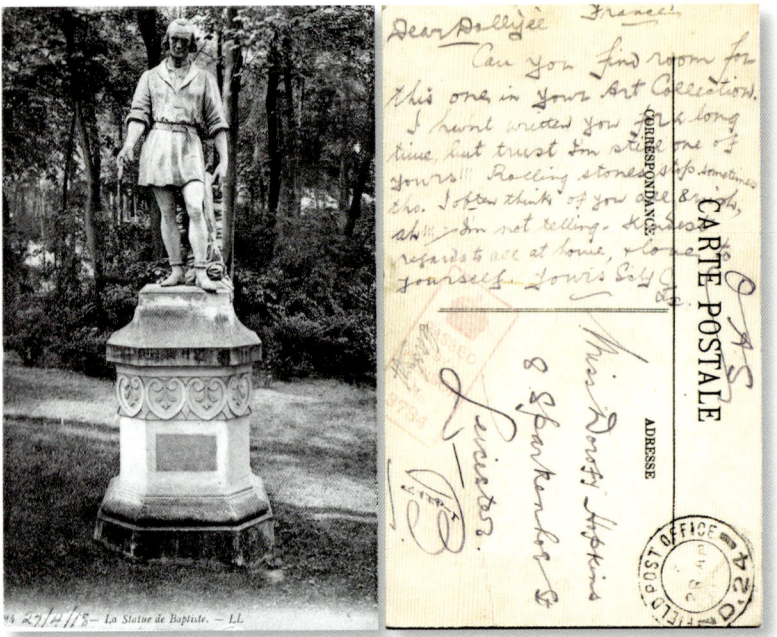

Postcard to 8 Sparkenhoe Street

One of those left disabled was Percy Hopkins, whose family lived in Sparkenhoe Street.

The 1911 census recorded the occupants at this address as sub-postmaster Thomas Hopkins, his wife Sarah Hopkins and their children Percy Thomas aged 18, Cicely Emily 17, Dorothy Louisa 14, and Herbert, 9. Percy, the older son, was employed as a railway clerk in Northampton at the time. He enlisted in November 1915 and joined the 3rd Battalion Northamptonshire Regiment in February of the following year. He was discharged in November 1917 as unfit for further service due to multiple gunshot wounds to his right thigh, which was amputated. He returned home on 23rd February 1917.

This postcard was sent to his sister Dorothy, by someone else: unidentified, but clearly a family friend. It was sent on 28th April 1918. The postmark indicates that it was from a unit within the 17th Division, a unit with no direct links to Leicester. At this date the great German offensive of March 1918 was grinding to a halt. Was this, perhaps, what the sender meant by "rolling stones stop sometimes tho"?

Some men joined the Royal Army Medical Corps, either because they already had some medical training or because they did not want to fight. Ten are recorded on the South Highfields street list. Someone not on the list was Herbert Orton[5] of Hanover Street.

"Sir Jonathan North, he got all the youngsters that were there, and I was one of them. 'Now lads, you will join the forces. England wants you.' Kitchener's finger pointing at you: 'It's you we need'. So of course we all went… I was not a fighter in that way, so I decided I wanted to be on the medical side and I joined the RAMC …They made us hospital ambulance transport…They put a gun on the back and we used to go all over the world…We went to Mudros to pick up the poor men that were being mown down at Cape Ellis - just mown down - and we used to bring them back to Malta."

Sir Jonathan North was Mayor of Leicester and in March 1915 became chair of the recruiting committee[6].

Mudros and Cape Ellis were part of the catastrophic Dardenelles campaign in 1915, fought on the Gallipoli peninsula in Turkey[7]. 13 of the 128 men listed died either in action or later of wounds. Many were injured.

Young lads marching, flanked by older men (Record Office)

The Soldiers

Mrs. Marston remembers her father:

"He was on the Somme and in Ypres, and he got badly gassed. He couldn't do a heavy job at all, although he lived for years, but he was an invalid."

Joseph Brown recalls his brother's experience:

"My brother had to join up, Arthur. In those days they got at you. 'We don't want to lose you, but we think you ought to go.' Arthur was 17. People would whistle the tune. He went through until February 1918 then he got shot to bits…Me mother used to worry. She never locked the door in case he came home from the front…He was a sniper. He survived. He'd got one eye and one arm. An awful mess, but he survived."

Wounded men arriving in Leicester (Record Office)

Doris Langham's brother was killed, following the death of another brother through illness:

"Jack, the oldest lad, he were called up and he was killed on October 2nd 1917 and that were the end of me mother. She died of a broken heart."

Anne Martin's father was also killed:

"My father joined up in First Leicester's Volunteers. With three children it wasn't necessary. It wasn't a call up, but he wanted to join up. I didn't see him again until September or October in 1916. He came home for a special Christmas leave, brought forward because they were expecting a big push on the Somme…I can remember him putting his flat soldier's hat on my head and dancing round the room with me… I was about four. He went back, and the next thing I remember, my sisters were at school and the telegram boy came. The front room was empty. I saw my mother walk over to the mantelpiece and put her head down on her hands, and I was tugging at her skirt which was long, to the ground. I understood then that my father had been killed and this was the telegram. Various things happened at school after that. Teacher used to say 'Stand up the children whose fathers have been killed in the war' and we were issued with tickets to go to De Montfort Hall for tea and presents."

Anne said she went to St. Peter's Girls' School, but she and her sisters were sent home on school church days[8] as they didn't have the right clothes for the crocodile march to the church. They only had black ribbons in memory of their father, and black three-quarter length socks. They couldn't afford school hats or black stockings.

The Soldiers

CONSCIENTIOUS OBJECTORS

The list also includes three known conscientious objectors, two of whom were put in the non-combatant corps. Most conscientious objectors were refused exemption, while others were granted it at their tribunal and put into the non-combatant corps or the service corps. Some then refused to obey military orders or do anything which helped the war effort. They were called absolutists, and sent to prison. Charles Kinton was an absolutist. He was not in the military records, but this page of an autograph book from Wakefield prison clearly gives his address in Myrtle Road. The autograph book belonged to conscientious objector William Joseph Poole from Desford[9].

Thomas Corder Pettifor Catchpool was a well-known conscientious objector. He was born on Saxe Coburg Street in 1883 but had moved away by the start of the war. He first joined the newly-formed Friends Ambulance Unit in France, but when conscription was introduced he returned and became an absolutist, spending the next two-and-a-half years in prison.

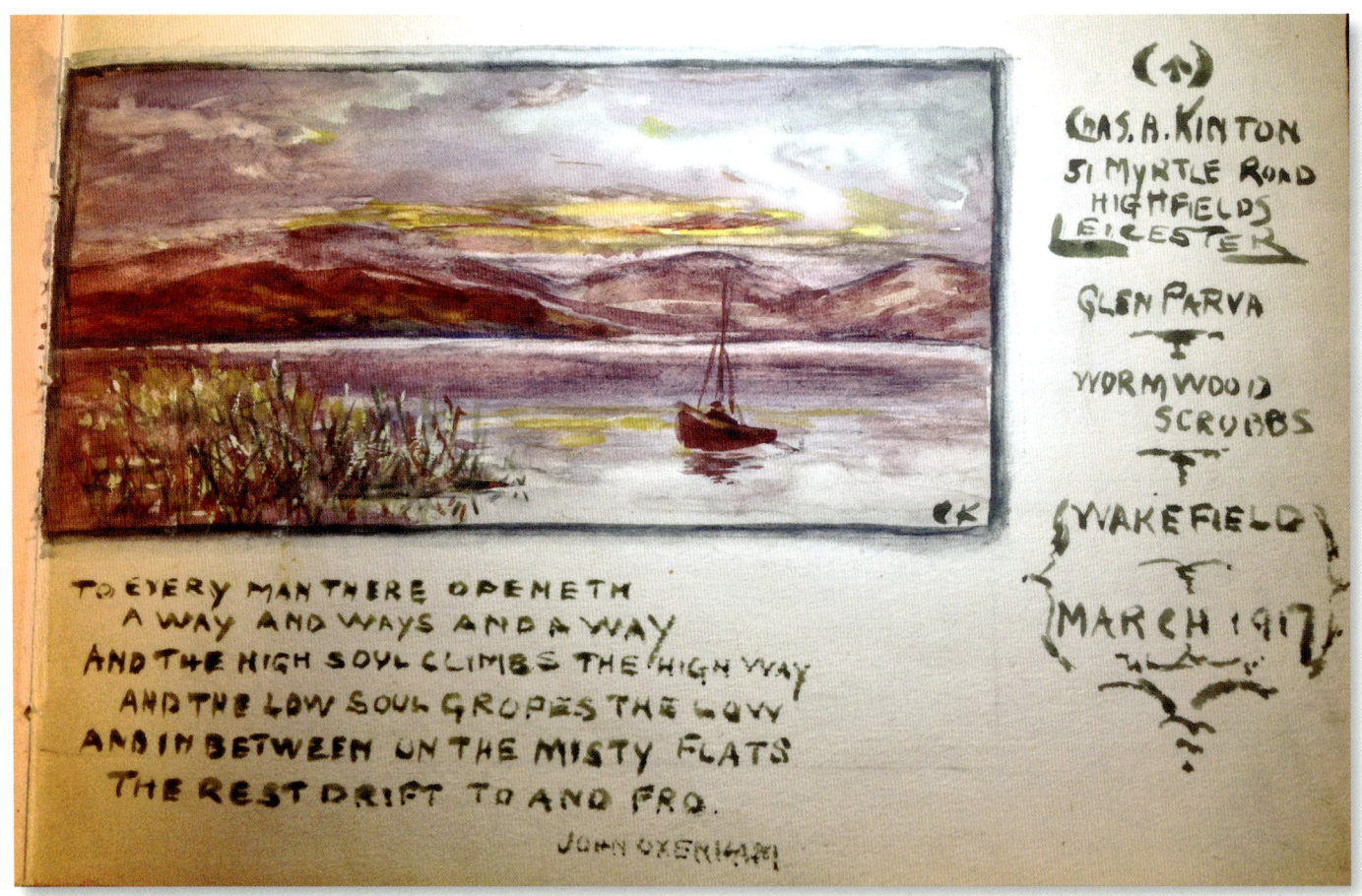

(Record Office)

The Soldiers

PRISONERS OF WAR

Prisoners of war had their own stories to tell.

Cyril John Daffern who lived at 7 Hanover Street enlisted in February 1917 when he was 18 years old. He was called up in March to serve in the Leicestershire Regiment 11th Training Reserve. He was then transferred to 8 Battalion South Staffordshire Regiment in September as private no. 45589, and was posted to France at the end of January 1918. On 2nd February he was transferred to the 2/6th Battalion South Staffordshire Regiment and was reported missing on the 21st March, having been captured by the German army after a fierce battle at Bullecourt on the Hindenburg Line. The regimental war diaries for 21st March state:

"Heavy enemy shelling of back areas commenced 2&3 am also heavy bombardment by enemy of Front and Support Line with HE and Gas Shells from 4 am-8 am. Enemy attacked in massed formation at 9 am and succeeded in capturing the front line and also effected a flank move and got though railway reserve and battalion HQ. 23 officers and about 600 O.R. are missing."

He was recorded as a prisoner of war on 12th June at Cassel POW camp along with others from his battalion, and then transferred to Chateau d'Oex, in Switzerland on 30th August for internment. He was repatriated on 6th December and was posted to No. 3 Depot, South Staffordshire Regiment on 10th February 1919. Cyril was finally discharged on 8th March 1919 as being "no longer physically fit for War Service due to Gunshot wound to left foot."

Cassel prisoner of war camp

Joe Wardle was one of those whose physical capacity was limited. He found it hard to find work after the War.

"When 1917 came and I was 18 I had to go to Wigston Barracks… and they said 'You go up to London'… I passed my trade and was sent to go into what was then the Royal Flying Corps, and I'd got to the station to go to Farnborough and the message came through - 'You've got to be 18½ to go into the Flying Corps.' They sent me home and I had to go to London the next day and took another test to go into motor transport, and there I stayed 'til 1919… I didn't go abroad. I wasn't of sufficient health to go abroad, being little… When I came home I didn't find any work for a long while. It was a terrible job being out of work in them days… I'd only been home three weeks and out of work, but still on leave and pay for a month, and women down the street were saying 'That so-and-so, he don't want any work--'."

HONOURING THE DEAD

Even before the War ended, temporary memorials were being erected in streets and churches. Several permanent ones survive in South Highfields. These can be seen in St. Peter's Church and St. James the Greater Church, as well as in the Synagogue and at Medway Street School. The memorial from the Wesleyan Chapel

St. James the Greater Church memorial

The Soldiers

on Saxe Coburg Street is now in Mayflower Methodist Church on Ethel Road, as the chapel was bombed in the Second World War. Sparkenhoe School was built on the site and incorporates what was left of the chapel.

Most major towns and cities, as well as many small villages, wanted to commemorate the sacrifice made by so many of their young men. Leicester was a wealthy city and wanted an impressive memorial. Edwin Lutyens was appointed to design it. He was an architect with an established reputation, having designed the imperial capital in New Delhi. He went on to design 133 cemeteries and war memorials around the world. The Arch of Remembrance in Victoria Park, so close to South Highfields, is a memorial, not a triumphal arch. It does not list the names of individual soldiers, but asks us to:

> "Remember in gratitude twelve thousand men
> Of this city and county who fought and died for freedom.
> Remember all who served and strove
> And those who patiently endured."

(Record Office)

When the Admiral of the Fleet, Earl Beatty, was unable to unveil the Leicester memorial, two local widows were found, who, between them, had lost six sons during the War: Elizabeth Butler and Annie Glover[10].

Leicester also commemorated the dead by establishing the Leicestershire and Rutland University College, (which in turn became the University of Leicester) on the site of the base military hospital, close to the memorial. University College opened in 1921. It took as its motto "Ut Vitam Habeant": That they may have life[11].

War memorial in Victoria Park
(photograph Dipak Mistry)

CHAPTER TWO | Life in South Highfields during the war

A hundred years ago, each street in South Highfields had a distinct social character. Richer residents lived in larger houses, typically toward the western end. Saxe Coburg Street is a good example. Poorer people lived in smaller houses to the east, like those in Laurel Road. This chapter takes these two streets as examples. More written records have survived for middle-class people, due to the nature of their work and social life. Oral history recordings of interviews with people who lived in South Highfields during the War mainly provide insights into working-class life. South Highfields was relatively prosperous. The worst poverty was found in other parts of Leicester, such as the Wharf Street and Abbey Street areas. What might appear now to be a very hard way of life was normal for most working-class people. The War had an impact on all social classes. For many it meant loss and hardship, but for some it brought new business opportunities and led to the growing employment of women.

PORTRAIT OF A STREET: SAXE COBURG STREET

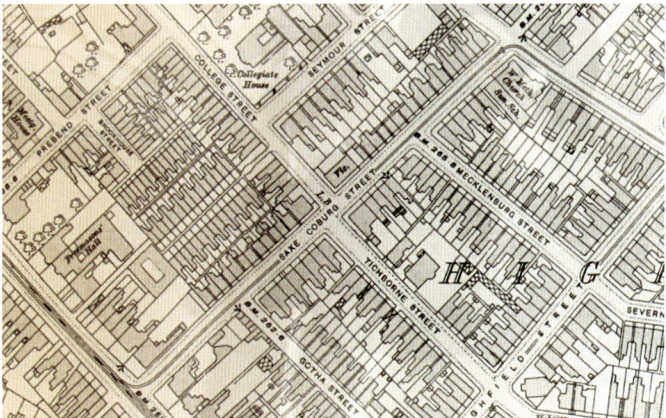

Most of the houses on Saxe Coburg Street had eight or nine rooms and at least one live-in servant was employed[12]. As well as residential properties the street included a Wesleyan chapel, a vicarage, an artificial teeth manufacturer, the offices of the Leicestershire Chess Club and a hostel for the shop assistants working for Joseph Johnson & Co Ltd. Johnson's were drapers, milliners and ladies' outfitters, with premises at the corner of Market Street and Belvoir Street. The building is now occupied by the Fenwick department store.

Saxe Coburg Street looking towards the Wesleyan Chapel (Record Office)

The houses on Saxe Coburg street were quite large and the residents there tended to be older. It was a place people moved to when they had established a career or company or had inherited money, and therefore there were few young families. One family, Wilfred Roberts and his wife and two grown-up children had gone up in the world, having moved from 2 Laurel Road to 10 Saxe Coburg Street. There were several houses occupied by widows, one of which was a boarding house until midway through the War. Of the nine men who served in the War, three were killed: Athelstan Webb, Bernard Stork and Arnold Keene.

The residents of Saxe Coburg Street were usually professionals or merchants. There were solicitors and surgeons, architects and musicians, a photographer, an ironmonger, tailors, a cigar manufacturer and other businessmen. Grown-up daughters were often employed as dressmakers, teachers or artists.

There were two members of the clergy. Reverend Cecil Robinson lived at St George's Vicarage, 28 Saxe Coburg Street, on the corner of College Street. He was

Life in South Highfields during the war

the vicar of St. George's Church in Rutland Street. He lived with his widowed mother and unmarried sister. The family were all born in County Cork, and employed three servants in their 13-room house. Reverend Robinson made a lively contribution to the newspaper debate about changing German street names. (see chapter three)

The other minister was Reverend Arthur Robert Ezard, who was the minister at the Congregational Church in Gallowtree Gate. He lived at 19 Saxe Coburg Street with his wife and three children. On 20th February 1905, while living in Dewsbury, Yorkshire he was sentenced to seven days in Wakefield Prison[13] for non-payment of rates. Many non-conformist ministers went to prison at this time including some in Leicester, because they refused to pay the education rate which funded Church of England and Catholic schools under the 1902 Education Act[14].

Several members of the Hebrew Congregation lived on Saxe Coburg Street. They included Jack Dorman at number 58 who was a tailor, and his wife Jane. They were both Russian Jews. Jack was born in Russia in 1878 and became a naturalised British citizen in April 1904 when he was living in Leeds. Their marriage in Leicester was announced in the Jewish Chronicle on 14th September 1906. Henry Simons, a tailor aged 43, lived at number 46 with his wife Rachel and their three children. He was also a member of the Hebrew congregation at the Synagogue in Highfield Street.

Frederick William Stork, a professor of music, lived at number 35 with his wife and three children. Frederick was born in London, but his father was a Swiss national. His youngest son, Bernard Stork, served as a private with the Leicestershire Regiment. He was killed in action on 13th October 1915, aged 18. His name is recorded on the Loos Memorial in France which commemorates over 20,000 officers and men who have no known grave. He is also remembered on the war memorial (panel four) in St Peter's Church, Leicester.

Synagogue memorial (photograph Andrew Thirlby)

Jacob Theodore Klee, a Catholic, was born in Frickhofen, Hessen, Germany in 1856. By 1889 he had emigrated to England and was living at 2 College Avenue. The 1891 census describes him as a British subject employed as a musician at the Royal Opera House in Silver Street, Leicester. By 1911 he was living at 22 Saxe Coburg Street with his wife, four children and a live-in domestic servant. A fifth child, 12-year-old Aloysius, was a pupil at a Catholic boarding school in Ratcliffe-on-Wreake. In 1925 Aloysius anglicised his name to Clay by deed poll. Two of Jacob's sons fought in the War and survived, although both were discharged before the end of the War as "no longer physically fit for war service", one because of "neurasthenia." This was a common diagnosis for stress during World War One. Soldiers who deserted their post could be executed, even if they were able to offer a medical reason for their behaviour. Officers with neurasthenia were not executed.

Life in South Highfields during the war

William Paulgrave Ellmore, a retired willow work manufacturer lived at number 23. He was a director of two hotels in Paris. He and his wife Mary had a total of ten children, seven of whom were still living in 1911. The family employed one servant. At the Royal Commission on Vaccination held in 1891 he was one of many prominent Leicester citizens to give evidence. He had been fined several times for refusing to allow his children to be vaccinated against smallpox[15]. During January 1897 William was granted the Freedom of the City of London as a member of the Company of Basket Makers. After the war in 1919 he wrote a book entitled *The Cultivation of Osiers and Willows*. When William died on 26th January 1933 he left an estate worth £59,960 5s 10d[16]. This would be worth about four million pounds today.

Charles Edward Keene
(Ned Newitt Radical Leicester)

Charles Edward Keene, his wife and nine children lived in the nine-room house at number 54. They employed a live-in servant. Charles was born in the Indian Ocean, on a sailing ship bound for India. His father was a regular soldier in the Indian Army and Charles was educated at an Indian army school. He returned to Britain in his late teens. Following the death of his father, his mother remarried, but his stepfather's excessive drinking brought ruin to the family. Charles was forced to sell newspapers on the streets of Bradford to supplement the family income. As a result he was a lifelong supporter of the Temperance Movement.

Charles and his family moved to Leicester in 1899 (reputedly with only six shillings in his pocket)[17] where he started businesses in box manufacturing and die stamping. He also set up the Mutual Clothing and Supply Company, a credit finance business. He later established Kingstone's store in Belgrave Gate. His third son, Arnold Victor Keene, served in the 7th Battalion Royal Fusiliers and was killed on 3rd April 1918, aged 19. The eldest son, Charles Robert Keene, left school at 14 and worked for his father. In 1910 he became a preacher at the Methodist church attended by the family, in line with his ambition to train as a Methodist minister. However, in 1914 he joined the Royal Army Medical Corps and served on hospital ships in the Mediterranean throughout the war. On his return he became the managing director of the Mutual Clothing and Supply Company and of Kingstone Ltd. He was elected to the Council in 1926 and served on many committees over the years. Charles Keene College of Further Education, now Leicester College, was named in his honour.

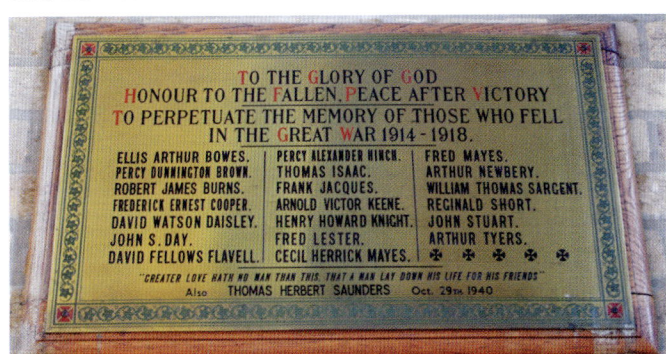

Memorial from Saxe Coburg Wesleyan Chapel showing Arnold Victor Keene
(photograph Andrew Thirlby)

Nearby Streets

Reverend Abraham Newman and his wife lived nearby at 16 College Avenue. He was the rabbi at the synagogue in Highfield Street from 1905 to 1939. He was born in Russia in 1871. His wife, Adeline, was also born in Russia in 1868. They had been married for 21 years at the outbreak of the War.

Life in South Highfields during the war

Harry Collins, described in *Wright's Directory of Leicester 1914* as a fish and game dealer, lived at 5 College Avenue with his wife and two daughters. He enlisted as a private in the 53rd Remount Squadron, Army Service Corps, on 25th September 1915 at the age of 41. He was discharged in February 1919, his papers marked "No longer physically fit for War Service". The ASC Remount Service was responsible for the provisioning of horses and mules to all other army units. They were generally older, experienced soldiers. Animals were bought by compulsory purchase in Britain and imported from North and South America, New Zealand, Spain, Portugal, India and China.

Fanny Fullager (Ned Newitt, Radical Leicester)

Kate and Fanny Fullagar lived at 20 Mecklenburg Street. They were the daughters of a local doctor. Fanny worked hard for the creation of Bond Street maternity hospital and for the training of midwives. In 1889 she became Leicester's first female Poor Law Guardian responsible for administering Poor Law provision, especially the large workhouse on nearby Sparkenhoe Street. A plaque outside the former registry office in Pocklingtons Walk remembers her today. Fanny was also a member of the Leicester Women's Suffrage Society which supported votes for women, but disapproved of the militant actions of local suffragettes. These included attacks on post boxes, telephone lines and railway stations. At Stoughton Drive golf course "no votes, no golf" was etched into the turf.

Andrew Weatherhead, a hosiery warehouse manager, lived next door to Fanny and Kate at 22 Mecklenburg Street. He was one of those who petitioned to have Mecklenburg Street given a less Germanic name. His son, Leslie Dixon Weatherhead, served in the Indian Army as a second lieutenant and later as a chaplain in the Devonshire Regiment. After his return to England in 1922 he became a well-known Methodist minister.

Clement Stretton and his family lived at 2 Mecklenburg Street in Saxe Coburg House. He was a civil engineer and railway author who, for a time, acted for ASLEF, the train drivers' union. His father had been Mayor of Leicester.

Saxe Coburg House (Record Office)

Frederick Mawby lived at 14, Mecklenburg Street (Bismarck Villas). He was a partner in the business of Buswell & Mawby, wood pulp merchants of Nichols Street.

Alexis Eduard Vivinus was living at 27 Mecklenburg Street in 1916. It is highly likely that this is the same

Life in South Highfields during the war

Alexis Eduard Vivinus who was born in Stenay, France in 1860 and married in 1902 at St. Josse Ten Noode, Belgium. His own company, Vivinus Cars, manufactured cars in Brussels. It also had a base in England. He later worked for Minerva, whose cars were used during the War for hit-and-run attacks against the Germans. Rifle and light machine guns were fired from minimally-protected, open-topped vehicles.

A member of the well-known Gimson family lived at 10 Mecklenburg Street. Joseph Yeomans Gimson enlisted in November 1915 and served in the 16th Battalion Tank Corps. He was the grandson of William Gimson, founder of W. Gimson & Sons, Timber Merchants. Other members of the Gimson family lived in the area. Henry Gimson lived at 11 College Street and Josiah Gimson at 90 Sparkenhoe Street. Sydney Gimson lived at 20 Glebe Street. He was the president of Leicester Secular Society[18] and chair of Leicester Town Council's Belgian Refugee Committee[19]. Henry and Joseph were involved in the family timber business, while Josiah and Sydney were working for the engineering company. Sydney's brother, Ernest, was the renowned Arts and Crafts designer and architect.

South Highfields was also the home of Ronald Light, who was tried for the infamous "Green Bicycle Murder". The 1891 census shows the family living in Seymour Street and in 1919, when the murder of 21-year-old Bella Wright was committed, he was living at 54 Highfield Street with his mother. Ronald had a troubled life. He was expelled from Oakham School in 1902, fired from his railway job in 1914 and lost his army commission in 1916. His father committed suicide the same year. He returned from the War, after re-enlisting as a gunner, partially deaf and with shell shock.

Despite strong evidence against Ronald Light he was acquitted.

LEFT Bella Wright (Leicester Chronicler)

RIGHT Ronald Light after his acquittal (unknown contemporary press photograph)

These are just some of the stories of people living in what were then the well-to-do streets of South Highfields. A number of people had moved to the area from another city, or even another country. The residents of Saxe Coburg Street and the neighbouring area were comfortably off. They are unlikely to have suffered from the food shortages and deficient wartime diet which people in poorer areas faced but nobody, rich or poor, escaped the terrible impact of the War.

 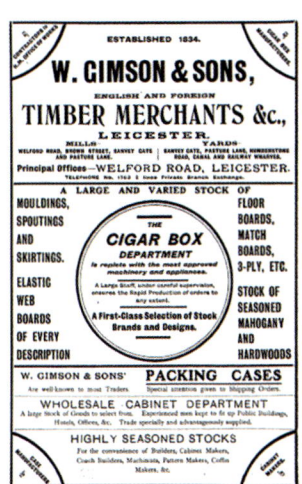

LEFT Sydney Gimson and his wife Jane photographed by Frank Brown who lived at The Limes, Saxe Coburg St

RIGHT White's Street Directory 1914

Life in South Highfields during the war

PORTRAIT OF A STREET: LAUREL ROAD

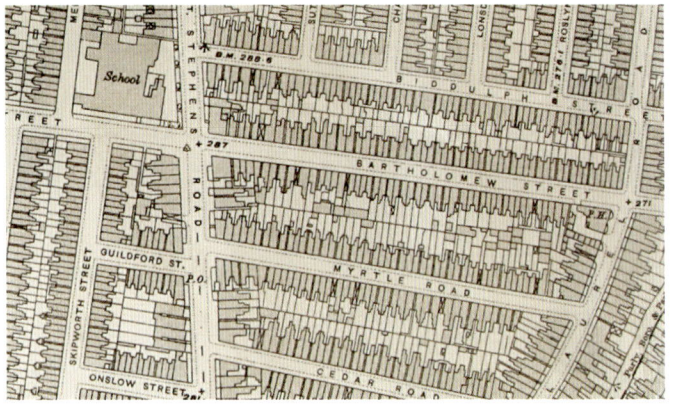

Laurel Road, on the other side of South Highfields, consisted of 118 houses extending from St. Peter's Road through to Evington Road. The terraced houses at the St. Peter's Road end, built in the 1880s, were small and housed a working-class community. Front doors opened straight off the street into a front-room parlour. Beyond that was a kitchen with a coal-fired range fitted into the wide chimney breast. The room now used as a kitchen was, in those days, a scullery with a sink and cold water tap. A copper boiler in the corner heated the water for wash day. Upstairs there were two bedrooms with fireplaces but these fires would have only been lit if was very cold, due to the cost of fuel. A smaller room, just big enough to accommodate a bed, led off the back bedroom. In many houses this has now been converted to a bathroom. The back yards were originally shared by four houses, with a communal toilet. By 1915 however, most of the yards had been divided, with a toilet and a coal shed for each house.

More affluent people lived in the larger houses towards the Evington Road end of the street. These are mainly three-storey dwellings with more varied and imposing frontages, and names like Hampton Villa and Prospect House. Most have small front gardens.

Gas lamps supplied light in both houses and streets. With coal fires as the only means of heating and cooking, smoke pollution was considerable.

This 1914 photograph of a Leicester street demonstrates the effects of smoke (Record Office)

Laurel Road in 2014 (photograph Dipak Mistry)

Life in South Highfields during the war

▮ At home

"There wasn't a lot of comfort on wash day."

Margot Cliffe[20] lived in the area. Laurel Road housewives would have identified with her memories of domestic life in the war years:

"Women worked hard… Wash day must have been awful. Mother got up at 6 a.m. to light the fire under the copper, to get water hot in time to start after breakfast. Clothes had to be dollied in a zinc tub with a thing like a six-legged stool with a long handle, which was twisted backwards and forwards to agitate the clothes. Whites were boiled in the copper and put through the mangle to get the water out. This was a big iron contraption with wooden rollers which were turned by a big handle…Try as you might, a good deal of water finished on the floor… Clothes were heavier, too, in those days. Man-made fibres didn't exist. Everything was cotton or wool, which shrank in unskilled hands…Ironing was done with flat irons, one heating up while the other was in use. There was nowhere much though, to get things dry, just a very much enclosed back yard where it must have been difficult to prevent things blowing onto dirty walls. On wet days the sheets would be dried in the entry. They can't have kept very clean as they touched the wall, but they got the heat from the chimney. Lines were strung up near the ceiling where airing clothes were hung. There wasn't a lot of comfort on wash day. There was no vacuum cleaner, not even a carpet sweeper. Fortunately our only carpet in the 'front room' was hair cord. This was swept with a dustpan and stiff brush. There was a lot of work on hands and knees. Lino and the kitchen red-tiled floor were scrubbed, and the living room lino was polished by hand. Of course, coal fires made a lot of work. Dusting daily was really necessary and curtains got dirtier than they do today. Grates, too, had to be black-leaded.

Standards were not as high as they are today. It would have been impossible to cope with clean stockings and pants daily, or frequent baths. Once a week was considered adequate. Heavy clothes like skirts, school tunics and coats were neither washed nor sent to the cleaners. Occasionally they would be sponged over with ammonia and water. Paintwork was always dark so that it need not be washed, and redecorating was very infrequent, and wallpapers got dark with age and smoke."

Census returns from 1911 provide a fascinating picture of those who lived in Laurel Road in the years just before the First World War. Street directories for 1914 and 1916 indicate that many of these families remained in the street during the War, although most houses were rented rather than owner-occupied, so there was some turnover of tenants.

The census records place of birth. Everyone living in Laurel Road had been born in Britain with the exception of one man who had come to Leicester from New Zealand. Many of the adults originated from the villages and small towns around Leicester, and may have moved to the city to find employment.

Very few people lived alone and some of the dwellings at the poorer, northern end of the street were significantly overcrowded. The Grants at number 37 had seven children, and several other families had six. Most of the houses were occupied by married couples, sometimes sharing with a widowed parent or other relatives. There were 20 widows in Laurel Road but only one widower, reflecting the lower life expectancy of men. Families tended to be quite large, with households of usually three or more children. Half the households would have experienced the death of at least one child[21]. Unmarried sons and daughters often continued to live at home, and several houses had lodgers. At the more affluent end of Laurel Road, however, six families had live-in domestic servants.

Life in South Highfields during the war

▋ At work

"The only holidays were a week for August Bank Holiday and two days at Christmas and Easter"

In 1911 about 200 people living in Laurel Road were employed. Very few married women went out to work. Those who did were from the poorer families. However, many single women, including older spinsters or widows were employed, particularly those in the less affluent families. Jobs such as teaching and nursing, dressmaking or domestic service were open to them, as well as some factory and shop work. The census information is recorded before the War and it is likely that many more women, married or otherwise, would have worked during the War.

In 1915 the situation had changed as described by Matthew Richardson in *Leicester in the Great War*

"Women were to become an increasingly common sight, working in many different industries and trades. As well as donning overalls in munitions and engineering factories, they could now be found working, for example, in banks as cashiers and as booking clerks at the railway stations (with lower class women undertaking the dirtier tasks, as engine and carriage cleaners in the sheds)." [22]

Betty Kendall's family were struggling for money, as all their savings had gone on the spiralling cost of food during the war:

"My mother was offered a job…she'd got a baby boy… It was in a factory which smelt to high heaven for miles around, which made stiffeners with all these glues and things…She took a job there and we had to look after the kids as best we could, while mother went to work."

Ellen Norris worked in the

"Standard Engineering Company in the munitions…big pieces of cast iron…had to file it down to the length of the shell…My sister worked at the back of me… We got 24 shillings a week…Working conditions were

Window cleaners (Record Office)

Local munitions factory, company unknown (www.worldwar1postcards.com)

Life in South Highfields during the war

jolly...There were only women in my room...There was another room where there were men...I'd got a boy of four, and he used to come and stand at the window watching us work. He used to stay there hours, watching us work".

Sometimes women took in washing or sewing to earn money. Hilda Stacey's mother

"cooked for a woman in Conduit Street every day for a shilling a week for 20 years"

although at that level of pay it amounted to neighbourly kindness, rather than a job.

In 1911 only a few men in Laurel Road were unemployed or retired. Children leaving school found work as errand boys, office boys or factory workers. Professional people living in the larger houses included a police superintendent at number 59, a physician and surgeon at number 84 and shop managers at 98 and 94. Those with smaller incomes lived at the other end of the road. People generally worked locally. Tradesmen included painters and decorators, gas fitters, builders and carpenters as well as a blacksmith, a cycle repairer and an organ builder. There were at least three corner shops in the road, selling fruit, vegetables and groceries. The Highfields Hotel near the corner of Bartholomew Street employed two barmen, a potman and a waitress, all of whom lived on the premises, along with the manager and his family. More than 50 people were employed in the garment industry. Some worked in the factories as machinists, menders or pressers, others as dressmakers, tailors or in the drapery shops. The boot and shoe trade provided work for at least 20 Laurel Road residents. These included clickers (who cut out the leather uppers for shoes), heel attachers and shoe finishers. Both the garment and the footwear industry employed managers, salesmen, foremen, bookkeepers, clerks, caretakers, warehousemen and shop workers. Some of these lived in Laurel Road. Local engineering firms serviced the machinery and they, too, employed people from the street.

Margot Cliffe describes typical conditions in the factories:

"Men worked a 48-hour week. Dad started at 7.30 and finished at 5.45 with 1 ½ hours for dinner ...most men lived near enough their work to get home for dinner... and of course he worked on Saturday mornings. He walked to and from Palfreyman's (a firm making shoes) in Dorothy Road. It must have been hard, as he stood all day and in later years, when he developed rheumatoid arthritis, it must have been very hard indeed. The only holidays were a week for August Bank Holiday and two days at Christmas and Easter. There was no pay during the holidays."

Benjamin Russell Factory on Eastern Boulevard 1918 (Record Office)

With the outbreak of war both the footwear and the garment factories were quickly pressed into service, making uniform and boots for the troops. The factories in the St. Saviours Road area, where some of the Laurel Road residents were likely to have worked, supplied the army with goods such as torpedo tube sights, searchlight mirrors, binoculars, razors and typewriters. For those who didn't go to fight there was plenty of employment.

Life in South Highfields during the war

▌ Laurel Road joins up

"April 1918: died of wounds"

The 1911 census lists two men who were already members of the armed forces. John Mathew Beese, the stepson of Arthur Rayner at 31 Laurel Road enlisted in October 1907 and was serving on HMS Dominion in 1911. During the War he served on several ships. He died in 1947, having also fought in the Second World War. Leonard Venables was part of a family of four unmarried brothers and a sister who lived at 60 Laurel Road. He enlisted in 1906 and was a lance corporal with the Coldstream Guards. He was killed in action in Flanders on 12th April 1918, aged 28. [23]

Military records [24] list seven others who enlisted:

From the 1911 census it is possible to identify 50 households where men and boys could have been eligible for military service. It is possible that a number of Laurel Road residents who worked in the garment, engineering and shoe industries were exempt, but there must have been many homes where the arrival of call-up papers was dreaded. Most of those who signed up did so in December 1915 or January 1916, when there was a lot of pressure from the Government and the threat of conscription. Some men may have served in the forces, but their military records have been lost. What is certain, however, is that the lives of everyone in the street would have been touched by the War.

House number	Name	Enlisted	Discharged
21	George Edgar Bates	December 1915, aged 22: Durham Light Infantry 6th battalion and 5th (reserve) battalion	December 1919
23	Benjamin Wilson	December 1915, aged 25: Royal Garrison Artillery, 160 and 117 Heavy Battery Royal Engineers	April 1918 : died of wounds
35	Albert Ernest Roberts	January 1916, aged 18: Durham Light Infantry Labour Corps	March 1919
49 (Highfields Hotel)	Frank Percy Warner Garner	January 1916, aged 25: Royal Engineers	February 1919
62	George Donald German	September 1915, aged 18: Royal Army Medical Corps	February 1919
72	Reginald Sarson	September 1915, aged 30: Leicestershire Regiment: Lincolnshire Regiment 12th battalion: Royal Army Medical Corps	September 1919
93	Percy Charles Laundon	December 1915, aged 23: London Regiment,15th (Co. of London) Battalion: Army Service Corps	Seriously wounded in the leg in France in 1916. Discharged 1919.

Life in South Highfields during the war

Shops and services

"All the streets...had a pawn shop."

Laurel Road is close to St. Stephens Road which has always been lined with shops, especially towards the Evington Road end. The street directories for 1914 and 1916 list a variety of shops and businesses, most of which continued to trade throughout the War years. There were two chemists, two drapers and a cycle repairer. The local post office was on the corner of Onslow Street. The Directories record that the post box was emptied 12 times a day and twice on Sundays. There was an office receiving parcels for both the Midland Railway and the London and North Western Railway. The same building is now called Global Communications Centre. It is still used to receive parcels and also to send money abroad. A hairdresser at number 59, a tailor at 52 and a launderer at 46 provided other local services. The tradesmen also included a joiner, plumber and painters. Two drapers supplied fabric, needles, pins and other sewing requirements at a time when many people made their own clothes. Many of the shops sold food, and unlike today's supermarkets, tended to specialise in a particular commodity. Kelly's Street Directory for 1914 lists three grocers (one of whom also sold wine and spirits), a confectioner and two fruiterers. Meat came from specialist shops, too. For example, shoppers visited the poulterer for poultry. There was also a fishmonger and two butchers, with one specialising in pork products. There were corner shops throughout Highfields and shops along Evington Road.

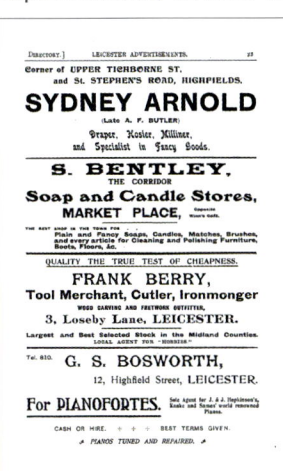
(White's Street Directory 1914)

Sidney Coleman remembers:

"At the corner shop everything was sold loose - sugar, vinegar, milk, butter, cheese, jam, treacle, bacon, lard, sweets - all wrapped up in a little bit of paper."

The Ordnance Survey map of 1915 shows that the tram network had recently been extended along East Park Road and up Evington Road to London Road. The people of South Highfields therefore had a good choice of local shops, as well as quick access to shops in the city centre. With no refrigerators or freezers, shopping for perishable items like meat and fish needed to be done daily. Some food shops would also deliver goods to the door. Milk was sold by local dairies from carts taken around the streets. Kirby and West had a depot on Hanover Street. The business began in 1861 when Thomas Kirby traded as a cowkeeper from Chatham Street, but in 1868 it became Highfields Dairy and moved to newly-built Hanover Street. The photograph shows Mr. Kirby with family and staff outside their dairy in 1892. In 1916 the dairy's milk sales were 250 gallons a day. The dairy moved to Western Boulevard in 1934. Today, Kirby and West no longer process milk, but still deliver daily to 25,000 households in Leicester.

Mr Kirby with family and workers outside Highfields Dairy in Hanover Street
(thanks to Kirby and West for this image)

Life in South Highfields during the war

Pawnbrokers offered a much-used service. They gave loans on deposited possessions which could then be bought back for a higher price. They were an important source of credit for working-class families.

Hilda Stacey remembers:

"All the streets in Leicester had a pawn shop"

and Sidney Coleman:

"There was a large pawnbrokers on Conduit Street by the name of Issitts, and mothers used to take their children's clothing, cleaned and pressed, on Monday morning and also the father's suit, which was fetched out on Saturday afternoon when he'd finished his work."

FOOD

"Me other sister was a professional queuer."

When War broke out the country was very dependent on imported food. Britain was the world's single largest importer of wheat, with its imports amounting to three-quarters of the combined amount purchased by Belgium, Italy, France, Holland, Switzerland and Brazil.[25] In the case of sugar more than half of the country's sugar was produced from beet sugar grown in Germany and the Austro-Hungarian Empire, the very countries with whom Britain was at war.[26] Even in the case of meat, although the country was famed for its high quality livestock, imports still accounted for nearly 40% of the total consumption.[27] It was only in heavy, bulky, low value commodities such as potatoes or perishable products like milk that the country was virtually self sufficient. However, imports of milk-based produce such as cheese and butter still amounted to more than 65% of total consumption.

In 1914 Britain's navy was more powerful than Germany's, hence the Government considered initially that there was little need to increase domestic food production as imported food would still get through. The British naval blockade of German ports started immediately the War began and continued after the War had finished, causing much hunger and suffering for the German people. In February 1917 the German navy started attacking all merchant vessels in 'unrestricted submarine warfare' when any shipping might be sunk without warning.[28] Feeding the population then became a major concern for the British Government.

The start of the war saw panic buying. On 5th August 1914 the *Leicester Daily Mercury* ran an article headed "No Fear of Famine, reassuring statement by the Government". It stated that there was a four-month supply of food in the country, and more consignments were on their way. "There is no justification for

Taken in 1918 in nearby Waterloo Street (Record office)

Life in South Highfields during the war

any present increase in the cost of meat or bread". However food costs spiralled. By early 1915 the cost of sugar had risen by 100% and many cereals by 50%.[29]

It wasn't just imported food which was hit by war. As many farm workers went off to fight, home production also became a problem. Following the bad harvest of 1916 the British government took more control over what farmers could grow, and tried to convince people to grow more themselves and eat less. Rationing wasn't formally introduced until January 1918, when sugar was rationed. By the end of April meat, butter, cheese and margarine were added to the list. Ration cards were issued and everyone had to register with a butcher and grocer.

The internment camps, holding prisoners of war and German civilians on grounds of national security, provided an alternative source of farm labour. There were many such camps in Leicestershire, as shown on the map in chapter three. The Women's Land Army also played a key role. As with the Voluntary Aid Detachment nurses caring for injured soldiers, it was mainly better-off single women who joined up to help on the farms. They received this government guidance:

"You are doing a man's work and so you are dressed rather like a man; but remember that because you wear a smock and trousers you should take care to behave like a British girl who expects chivalry and respect from everyone she meets." [30]

There were 20,000 women in the land army by 1918.

Allotments were already in use when war broke out, and in 1917 Leicester Borough Council[31] encouraged residents to spot unused land and apply to use it to grow vegetables. Within three months, 90 acres of unused land and 77 acres of occupied land had been identified, including areas in parks. These were allocated rent-free for growing food.

"The Board of Agriculture offered to supply allotment societies seed potatoes to get them started ....in April 1919, 1,500 acres of land within the borough were under cultivation". [32]

The women's land army (Record office)

In order to encourage the population to grow more of their own food New Walk Museum held several exhibitions and talks about food in 1917 and 1918:[33]

February 1917	Food growing exhibition
Feb - April 1917	Food growing lectures: special war-time lectures by Mr. John Hudson
May 1917	Food economy exhibition (opened by Lady Beatty and attracting 100,000 visitors)
July 1917	Fruit bottling: wartime exhibition and demonstration by the Ministry of Food
February 1918	Garden Pests: three wartime lectures by Mr. Woolley
March - April 1918	Food producing and food saving exhibition

A small apiary was installed in the grounds of the Museum. The Curator investigated bee diseases, which were now so important because of the shortage of sugar.

Life in South Highfields during the war

The following first-hand reports of what food shortages meant in daily life come from oral history recordings of people who were children during the War.

Ellen Norris describes rationing carrying on

"for quite a while after the war ended. Half a pound of sugar a week, half a pound of butter, meat two ounces. You could get veg. and liver and offal and fish."

Betty Kendall has a different recollection:

"I remember a shortage of food…no rationing as there was in the Second World War…if you'd money you could get food, but you'd got to go and look for it."

Hilda Stacey's parents were better off, as her father was a policeman. Before the War:

"We had suet pudding, bread dipped in fat, everything fatty…but plenty of it…home-made cakes…egg custard…baked potatoes in the oven…we always had the trimmings."

But during the War:

"We nearly starved in the First World War…we had mashed potato on bread."

Hilda had two sisters:

"Me other sister was a professional queuer…she was younger than me…if they heard there was margarine being sold, Madge would go and queue. She'd do anything but go to school."

Queuing for food was a regular feature of life during the war.

Bread queue (Record Office)

Margot Cliff remembers:

"Some of my earliest memories were queuing with mother, before I went to school. I remember once queuing for what seemed like hours for butter at 'The Maypole', only enlivened by watching the assistant pat slabs of butter into pounds with two wooden patters. Mother was lucky when we moved to Mere Road to find a helpful butcher, Mr Bamford, at the corner of Conduit Street and Sparkenhoe Street. She stuck with him all her life."

Mrs Marston recalls:

"During the War, one day all we had was porridge, no milk, no sugar, just porridge with salt in it…It wasn't rationed. If you had the money, you could get it."

Life in South Highfields during the war

CHILDREN'S LIVES

"I was put in a Church of England home"

The effects of war could hit children hard, even if their father wasn't in the military. For example, Lawrence Woodward's father worked in a munitions factory, which made him ill. He died in 1918. Munitions work was dangerous and the chemicals caused skin to turn yellow, resulting in the nickname "canary women". Some women became infertile as a result. For the Woodward family, the father's death was catastrophic. His wife's health broke down and she was taken to live in a home for the next 15 years, until her daughter brought her out. The children were taken to children's homes and badly treated.

"I was put in a Church of England home in Avenue Road Extension, Clarendon Park with 30 boys, most of them orphans…Mr Munroe had been a petty officer in the war. He was a big man…Early morning, he was always in a violent temper. We had to do ablutions, and Munroe would come down those stairs and always find some excuse for sending someone sprawling."

▌Games

"Battledore and Shuttlecock on Shrove Tuesday"

Children played simple games a hundred years ago. Mrs Marston remembers:

"We used to swing on the lamp posts…We gave supposed concerts…We'd dress ourselves up."

Hilda Stacey:

"We used to play on those girders on Swain Street Bridge."

Swain St. Bridge (photograph Dipak Mistry)

Margot Cliff recalls:

"When we were children we didn't have many toys, but I don't think we missed them. We played 'schools' indoors. Shells sat on bricks with a large hosiery bobbin in front, to make a desk top. The pretty shells did beautiful work, but the plainer shells were villains. We spent as much time as possible playing out. The traditional games were still played: battledore and shuttlecock on Shrove Tuesday, whip and top, hoops,

Life in South Highfields during the war

marbles (for boys), but the main outdoor toys for girls were balls and skipping ropes. There were elaborate rituals for bouncing balls and cocking a leg over the ball, and for throwing balls up against a wall."

Top and whip

Sidney Coleman played a different game:

"A very rough game we used to play was called 'Releaso'. Several of you were one side of the street and your opponents the other. At the word 'go' you caught hold of each other and dragged him or his clothing to the other side of the street."

Margot on the right, with sister Gwen (thanks to Gillian Lighton)

"Hopscotch was played on the six squares of paving slabs with a ball, and other types with a spiral chalked on the road, or with a stone on a pavement with the slabs differently laid. Skipping was individual - plain, pepper and American jump (one jump to two turns) or communal. There were rhymes and systems for first end, etc. and for turns. Roads were quiet, and many games were played in the middle of the road. Occasionally I remember playing the round singing games described in 'Larkhill to Candleford'. These survived in the poorer streets between Mere Road and Medway Street School."

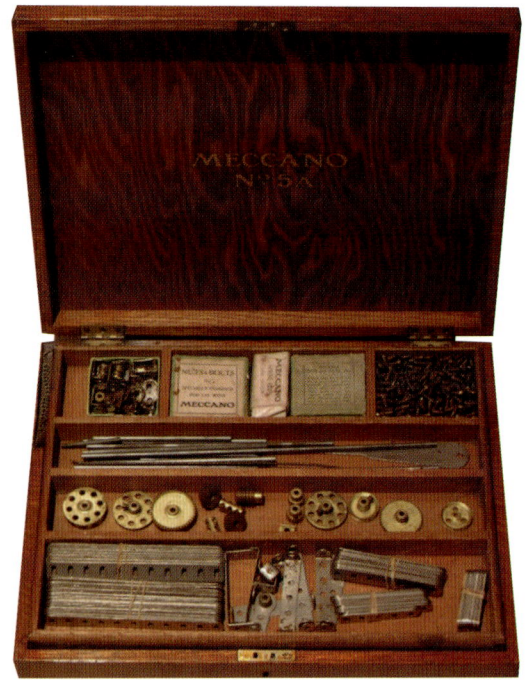
Meccano may well have been found in wealthier houses. Invented in 1900 and named 'Meccano' in 1907 it was a popular game. This is the 1917 outfit 5a.

Life in South Highfields during the war

■ School days

"I envied the children who hid under desks, and above all, in the cupboard".

Before the Education Act of 1918 the school leaving age was 12.[34] Children often had jobs while they were still at school.

Sidney Coleman was one of them:

"At the corner of Glebe Street and Conduit Street was a very fashionable milliner's… I'd run from Melbourne Road School at nights and take a band box with its leather strap and a beautiful ladies' hat in it up to Stoneygate; wait until the lady had tried it on and if it was OK, she'd say it was OK. If it wasn't OK she'd put a note inside and I'd run back with it."

Lillian Smith's family had a shop in Biddulph Street:

"I went to Medway Street…I was 10 when I left there…a big school, Medway Street. Our shop was at the top of Biddulph Street…It had a pickled onion jar and a pickled cabbage jar under the counter, and I used to bend down and get a pickled onion as I left for school…It was a nice school… I got lost in the fog once, coming home."

During the War, Medway Street School was the main elementary school for South Highfields. It is still a thriving school, but with half the number of children in the same-size building. In 2014 there were 473 pupils on the register; in 1914 there were 980. The head teacher at the time was Mr. G. Neighbour.

The school log book [35] tells us a lot about the profound impact the War had on the school. Extracts from the log book are shown in italics.

The first mention of the War comes in an entry for 29th September 1914: *A roll of honour is being compiled*

Medway School in 2014 (photograph Dipak Mistry)

in connection with the Great War and 146 names of former Medway Street boys have already been received. This roll would have recorded the names of former pupils who now served in the army.

In 1915 the school was taken over by the military to serve as a clearing station for wounded troops, and so the children moved out on 22nd March 1915 to the building which is now the Melbourne Centre. The school log book records: *At 11.00 the children were marched to the Melbourne Road Council School each child carrying a share of the stock.*

Margot Cliff didn't start school until 1916, but she remembers what happened to her older sister, Gwen:

"She says they all walked over carrying something. She had a box of knitting pins and despite being told not to open the box, she did, with catastrophic results."

Life in South Highfields during the war

With two schools now sharing one site, it was decided that the Medway Street children would attend from 9.00-12.30 one week and from 2.00-5.30 the following. This was altered to 2.00-4.00 during the winter months. Homework was introduced to compensate for the reduced hours of schooling. The log book entry for 22nd April 1915 reads: *The children are working willingly and the parents are supporting loyally.*

On 29th April 1915 details were given of the arrangements made for each teacher to devote at least one afternoon each week to outdoor work. Subjects to be studied included: *nature walks, practical field work (measuration and surveying), local history and geography, organised games and supervision in the parks.*

Some staff left. An entry for 29th November 1915 records: *Miss Humphreys left today to take up her work as a VAD nurse.* She may have worked locally at the Knighton VAD hospital. She returned to her teaching post for a short period, three and a half years later.

On 12th May 1916: *Mr. Harle left to join his regiment in Edinburgh.* He is mentioned again on 14th September 1916: *Mr. Harle was killed in France on the 3rd. He left here for training four months ago.* (Fred Harle served in the Royal Fusiliers. He died on the 4th September, not the 3rd, as stated in the school log book. He is commemorated at the Caterpillar Valley Cemetery, Longueval, France.)

Pages 181 and 182 of the school log book (Records Office)

Life in South Highfields during the war

Other staff had close family members in the forces. Mrs Salter was given a fortnight's holiday when her husband was home on leave from France. She had further leave of absence when he returned home at the end of the war.

Throughout the war, Medway Street children and staff contributed financially to alleviate some of the hardship created by the conflict. The log has details of the amounts and the causes for which they were raised. There were collections for the Alexandra Rose Day fund (which benefited London hospitals) and Flag Days to raise money for other charities. These included the Red Cross, the St. Dunstan's fund (for blinded war veterans), the Prisoners of War fund and the fund for Belgian refugee children. Money was also given to buy knitting wool, Christmas puddings and cakes. The sum total of the various donations came to £220 8/6½d. Today, this would be worth about £10,000.[36]

The school log proudly records the practical support given to the War effort. The older boys worked on the vegetable gardens in Victoria Park near the end of the War. The girls knitted articles such as socks, scarves, mittens and gloves for the troops, and items for the VAD hospital. Hundreds of gas masks and uniform sacks were made by the upper standard girls and teachers. They also helped at a local baby convalescent home and at day nurseries.

Children and staff were involved in some of the administrative work generated by the war. 100 children, assisted by all the teaching staff, attended the Corn Exchange in the market place. The National Registration Act of 1915 required every person aged 15-65 to complete a form giving details of their name, age, marital status, nationality and employment. The information about all men aged between 19 and 41 was copied onto pink forms which were handed over to the military for recruitment purposes. Medway Street children were involved in sorting these forms at the Assembly Rooms. Staff visited local streets to compile lists of voters. Voting cards for soldiers were written out by standard five children at the Town Clerk's office. When rationing was introduced in January 1918, the children wrote out the ration cards for sugar under the supervision of various members of staff.

Margot Cliff remembers:

"In the final stages of the War we had preparation for air raids. We all had a place. I merely stood in a corner. I envied the children who hid under desks, and above all, in the cupboard."

During 1918 parents expressed anger about the disruption to their children's education. A letter to the *Leicester Mercury* on 3rd September 1918 states:

"In March 1915 the children brought home to their parents a printed notice to say that all children attending these two schools would, in future, have to attend the Melbourne Road school, and that they would only have to attend once a day instead of twice a day. These children have now been attending half time for three years and five months, with the same holidays as children attending full time at the other Leicester schools. The parents of the children... consider the authorities are not treating the children or their parents at all fairly....During the war, sacrifices have got to be made, but is it fair that the children shall be compelled to sacrifice all that is essential to them and the nation, in the years to come?"
S.TAYLOR Worthington St.

And on the 5th September: "I quite agree with Mr. S. Taylor in regard to the children of this district who are spending the best part of their schooldays running around the streets, and some of the older ones working half time as errand boys. How can they expect them to learn in an afternoon when they have been pushing a truck about all morning?...Need one wonder if the children are backward?"
W.H GOODACRE Donington St.

Life in South Highfields during the war

From June 1918 there is frequent mention in the log book of the influenza epidemic sweeping the country. With 111 children absent through illness, the school closed early for the summer holidays in July. On 18th October the school had to be closed as half the children and six members of staff had influenza. This closure carried on until 11th November, the day the war ended, when the log book simply reads:
Reopened school. Miss Warren and about 25% of the scholars absent.

The buildings were finally handed back to the education authorities. On December 19th 1918 the log book records: *At 11.10 the children were marched up to Medway Street School. Each child carried small parcels of stock. After giving up the stock to the teachers the students were dismissed for the Christmas holidays.*

Today, a plaque in the upstairs hall provides a reminder of the wartime years. It was unveiled by Sir Jonathan North in November 1920 and reads: "In honour of the old Boys and Teachers of this school who served in the Great War 1914–18."

HEALTH

"The horses came with the ambulance."

Influenza

Although many young children were ill and away from school in 1918 and 1919 the majority of people who died from influenza were not the young and the old, as is usually the case with epidemics, but people in their 20s and 30s. Sadly, these were sometimes men who had fought and survived the war only to succumb to influenza, while others returned to find their wives had died. It also affected many pregnant women.

An estimated two per cent of the population in Britain died from the Spanish flu outbreaks of 1918 and 1919. Between 2nd February and 15th March 1919, 824 people died in Leicester of influenza and associated illnesses.[37] It is difficult to identify the number of people affected in South Highfields. We know of one young man - John William Claypole from 8 Laurel Road - who died when he was 17 and was buried by the funeral directors James and Son at Welford Road Cemetery on March 29th 1919. The account from his

Medway Street School memorial (photograph by Andrew Thirlby)

Billy Claypole, as he was known, with his milk cart (thanks to Alan Craxford)

Life in South Highfields during the war

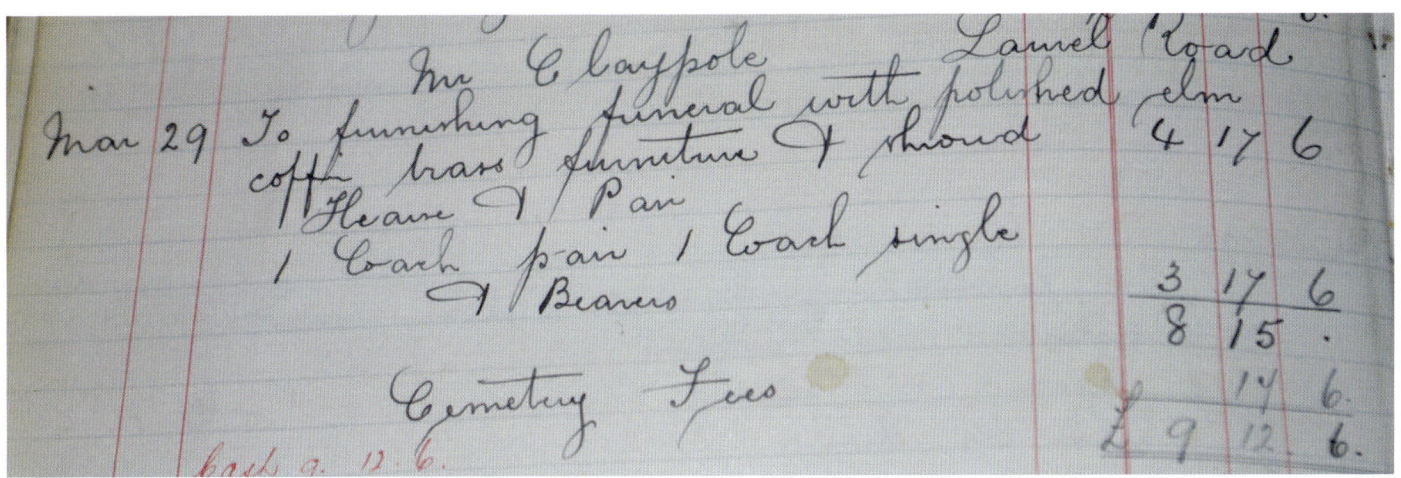

Page from the ledger of A. C. James and Sons Funeral Directors showing Billy's funeral costs (photograph Andrew Thirlby)

funeral is taken from their ledger. His family have a website[38] from which this photograph was taken. He worked for Flowers Dairy in Mere Road.

Records of burials at Welford Road Cemetery[39] for the streets in South Highfields between 1914 and 1919 show a marked increase during 1918 and 1919, (the years of the influenza epidemic) for the most vunerable age group. Some of these may have been returning soldiers who died of their injuries. Not everyone was buried there. Jewish people, for example, had bought a section of their own in Gilroes Cemetery in 1902, but most South Highfields residents would have been buried at Welford Road Cemetery. This is confirmed by the records of A C James and Son.

	1914 -1917 (4 years)	1918 -1919 (2 years)
6 - 10 year olds	1	6
11 - 20	11	11
21 -30	10	20
31 -40	14	16
Total 36	Total 36	Total 53
	(average of 8 per year)	(average of 26 per year)

South Highfields burials at Welford Road cemetery 1914 -1919 showing increase in deaths of people aged 6-40 in 1918 and 1919 probably because of the flu epidemic

The influenza pandemic sweeping the world was only one of many health problems faced by the people of South Highfields. There was no National Health Service. The rich were able to pay doctors' fees and buy medicines, but without a free health service poorer people avoided doctors and their fees until absolutely necessary. Some doctors were prepared to treat those unable to pay. Home remedies were popular. There were some insurance schemes connected to work, but they were far from universal.

Hilda Stacey remembers:

"You paid so much a week and the man called for the money…You went to the doctor free…and when you got your paper you went to the dispensary and got your medicine."

Anne Martin remembers being ill as a child:

"There was an epidemic of diphtheria. There were seven in the street with it… Doctor Cooper came. He lived at the top of Highfield Street… I had to drink castor oil and orange juice but it didn't work… The horses came with the ambulance to take me to the isolation hospital. They had to stop for a rest half way… The seven children, none of them died…I was nearly unconscious for two weeks before I got better."

Life in South Highfields during the war

▌Infant mortality

Further analysis of the burial records at Welford Road Cemetery for the streets in South Highfields shows a high level of infant mortality, especially in the first year. The table below shows children's burials during the War years from 1st August 1914 to 30th November 1918 at Welford Road Cemetery.

Total burials:	425
Children up to and including 15 years of age:	97 (22.85% of total burials)
Age groups of children: Stillborn	15
Lived for 24 hours	10
Up to 1 year	47
1 to 5 years	13
6 to 10 years	6
11 to 15 years	6
Total:	97

South Highfields burials at Welford Road cemetery 1914 -1918 of children aged 15 and under showing high level of infant mortality

32 of these burials, nearly one third, came from Mill Hill Lane where there was a children's home which had been opened as a 'receiving home' in July 1908. It catered for sixteen boys and sixteen girls who were entering Poor Law Union care, and gave them medical checks before passing them on to one of the Union's cottage or scattered homes. The premises later became The Oaks boys' home. The Lodge in Mill Hill Lane provided a home for 20 'ins-and-outs': children who were frequent short-term residents.

Six of the 97 burials originated from 14, Welland Street, which in 1916 was the home of a midwife, Mrs Alice Elizabeth Howe (but not in 1914, when no burials originated from that address.)

To reduce infant deaths, New Walk Museum put on an *"Infants' Welfare Exhibition"* in December 1915. The Museum report[40] states "With the voluntary assistance of experts, an exhibition dealing with feeding, clothing, and the general welfare of infants was arranged. It had a very successful run and was copied by several other museums".

New Walk Museum is close to South Highfields and it is likely that some South Highfields residents visited the exhibition. Voluntary health visitors were notified of all new births, and continued to visit mother and baby at home for 12 months. They didn't visit the "better-class" homes[41], probably so that they could concentrate their efforts on wards with the highest levels of infant mortality.

Dr Charles Killick Millard was the Medical Officer of Health. Rather than blaming mothers for their "ignorance and carelessness", Millard argued that poor housing and poverty were responsible for the high levels of infant mortality. On average in Leicester between 1912 and 1916 there were 115 deaths of infants under a year old, per 1,000 births. This number rose to 224 deaths in poorer areas and fell to 22 in the outer areas[42].

Welford Road Cemetery (photograph Dipak Mistry)

Life in South Highfields during the war

■ Lower life expectancy in some streets

The number of deaths fluctuated within South Highfields as this table demonstrates. Skipworth Street was in the poorer area, with smaller terraces housing a working-class community. Burial records show that life expectancy there was much lower than the average for South Highfields as a whole.

	All streets in South Highfields	Skipworth Street
Stillborn	20 3.4%	2 9.6%
0-5	90 15%	4 19.2%
6 - 10	7 1.3%	0 0%
11-20	22 3.8%	0 0%
21-30	0 5%	5 24%
31-40	30 5%	1 4.8%
41-50	38 6.4%	1 4.8%
51-60	69 11.5%	3 14.4
61-70	106 18%	2 9.6%
71-80	105 18%	2 9.6%
81-90	66 11.2%	1 4.8%
91 +	8 1%	0 0%
Total	591 (99.6%)	21 (100.8%)

South Highfields burials at Welford Road Cemetery 1914-18 showing age of death in Skipworth Street compared to average age of death for the whole of South Highfields

In Skipworth Street 62.8% of burials were of people aged 30 and under. For that age group, the average for the whole area was 28.5%.

■ Drink, disease and moral panic

"tin-panned out the street"

During the War there was an element of moral panic, fuelled by newspapers, about 'patriotic' women keen to give soldiers a 'good time' before they went to war. Concern that soldiers would return to the front with venereal disease led to the Defence of the Realm Act 1914, which made it a criminal offence for a woman with VD to solicit or have intercourse with a man[43]. Some thought, with little evidence, that women who were working while their men were away at the front would spend their money on alcohol.[44] Drinking was also seen as a problem for soldiers home on leave and for factory workers, and so the Defence of the Realm Act closed pubs at 9 pm from 1st January 1915.[45] The YMCA near the Midland railway station offered a shelter to soldiers getting off the train, to keep them free from women and alcohol.[46]

Hilda Stacey remembers:

"If you lived with anyone else, like they do today, they were tin-panned out the street...everybody got saucepan lids and banged them."

■ Coping with birth and death

"They needed the money to bury him".

In the poorer areas there would be someone in the street who helped deliver babies and laid people out when they died.

Ellen Norris's mother was one such woman:

"People would fetch her for bringing children into the world and laying people out what had died. She'd go out all times, as God sent".

Anne Martin's mother also did this work:

"Mother laid people out and she delivered babies...She could never turn a tramp away from the door...One morning I woke up and ran into her bedroom, and she said 'Look in that box there'...It was a baby...It looked navy blue. It was a woman that lived in the same street.

Life in South Highfields during the war

She was an epileptic. My mother brought it home and looked after it but it died. It wasn't a paid job. If you could do it, you did it."

Death was very much a part of life here, as it was on the battlefields. Most deaths happened at home rather than in hospital. When someone was dying, it was customary to lay peat or straw over the cobbled streets to reduce traffic noise.

Mrs Marston remembers:

"In our street was cobbles and also a lot of dray horses, and so anyone who was dying, the corporation came and put down a thick layer of peat to deaden the noise."

The body stayed in the front room in a coffin until the funeral, and friends and neighbours would visit. Children were encouraged to take part in the ritual of visiting. Local historian Cynthia Brown writes

"One local woman remembered paying a penny to see the body of another child in an accident. The family 'had him in the front room in a little coffin…I suppose they needed the money to bury him'..Most of the children went…It was better if the first dead body you saw wasn't one of your own family. It wasn't so shocking…At a child's funeral it was the custom to wear white gloves, symbolising - like the traditional white coffin itself - the innocence and purity of the young life prematurely ended…Black clothing remained the custom for other funerals…However, many working-class families…would make do with a black armband, or a diamond of black fabric stitched to a sleeve." [47]

Horse-drawn hearses were used until the middle of the 1920s. This is a photograph of A.C. James and Son, the undertakers who buried William Claypole and who are still busy in Biddulph Street today.

(Thanks to A.C. James and Son Funeral Directors)

CHAPTER THREE | Why the street names were changed

This chapter looks at laws affecting Germans living here during the War, and at the anti-German attitudes which led to changes in some street names in South Highfields.

Two local residents - Herr Baumeister and Herr Richter - provide good examples of the treatment of Germans at that time. The press were not slow to stir up anti-German feeling when reporting events like the sinking of the *Lusitania* in May 1915. Public feeling was also aroused by the sight of wounded soldiers going to and from the nearby hospital, and of news of family and neighbours being killed or injured. With the names of German composers and musicians erased from concert programmes at De Montfort Hall, it is not surprising that German names were also removed from local streets.

In the late nineteenth century substantial German communities were established in Britain, and in 1911 there were more than 53,000 German people living here. Some were classed as 'aliens', meaning they did not live in their home country. Others had applied for British citizenship and had been 'naturalised'. In 1911 there were 92 Germans and 36 Austrians living in Leicester who had not been naturalised. This was very few compared to cities like London, Manchester and Liverpool. Newspapers abounded with sensationalist stories about spies and conspiracy, which only served to spread fear and suspicion. One and a quarter million people gathered at a meeting in Hyde Park, demanding that all enemy aliens be interned. The government gave in to this pressure with harsh and probably unnecessary measures.[48] Germans – naturalised or otherwise – were under permanent suspicion. They had to register with the police, and if the authorities considered them to pose a threat they were placed in internment camps.[49] The government required all foreign nationals to register with the authorities and keep them informed of any change of address, on pain of substantial fines. Certain areas were proscribed, and aliens had to have permits to live there. They could not travel more than five miles from home, and their social institutions were closed down.[50]

The *Leicester Daily Post* of 8th August 1914 reported that about 50 aliens had been arrested and held at the Corn Exchange. Apparently 18 "reservists"[51] were found among them, who were classed as prisoners of war.[52] Others were released.[53] In September 1914 only 3,100 of the 13,600 internees had actually come from the battlefields. The order had been to round up all Germans and Austrians aged between 17 and 42 if they were considered dangerous.[54]

Why the street names were changed

INTERNING THE ENEMY

Many countries, including Britain and Australia, set up internment camps to hold German people and prisoners of war. The map shows the distribution of camps around the city of Leicester.

German officers were held at the Donington Hall camp at Castle Donington. The quality of their accommodation was better than that provided for ordinary soldiers. When prisoners were escorted through the town, large crowds came out to watch. This provided entertainment for the population, but must have been humiliating for the captured soldiers.

The *Leicester Daily Post* of 5th April 1916 reported that officers from the captured 'Zeppelin L15' which sank at the mouth of the Thames were taken to Donington Hall under military escort. The "three German officers - well-built, athletic-looking fellows" drew a large crowd.

German officers on their way to Donington Hall Camp (Record Office)

The newspaper claimed that "as the officers were marched through the streets, they appeared to feel their position very acutely. A crowd of children marching in the rear of the procession sang 'Rule Britannia'."

The story of a hairdresser

Maximilian Josef Baumeister was a German from Bavaria living in South Highfields in 1914. He lived at 28 College Avenue with his English wife Nellie and their daughter, who was born in 1912. Emily Violet Bateman, a hairdresser's assistant, also lived with them. She had been born in India and probably worked at the hairdressing salon which Baumeister ran at 75 Granby Street. Baumeister was taken to the Corn Exchange but later released. He was interned in December 1914. In August 1915 Baumeister was again interned and held at the prisoner of war camp in Handforth, Cheshire. In October 1918 he was transferred to the camp at Spalding. After the War, Baumeister returned to live at College Avenue and worked as a hairdresser until his death in 1928, after which his wife continued the business. Their German name does not appear to have affected trade, as it did in some areas.

Why the street names were changed

▎Willibald Richter

"I beg protest against my imprisonment"

Willibald Richter, also German, lived in South Highfields at 57 London Road. He was born in Germany in 1860. At the age of 20 he moved to England, and taught music at Uppingham School.[55] Richter married another master's daughter, Charlotte, in 1887. In 1904 Willibald became naturalised as a British citizen. He had a son, Siegfried, and a daughter, Charlotte. In 1911 their household had a cook and a housemaid.[56] Richter should have been looking forward to a comfortable middle age.

In the census of 1911 he described himself as a 'Professor of Music', by which he meant that he taught a number of private students.[57] Richter was well-regarded for his music, having been taught by Liszt.[58] He published Hints for the Systematic Study of Finger Exercises on the Pianoforte.[59] As well as composing various songs he was a pianist at the Proms, under the famous conductor Sir Henry Wood. He also set up the Leicester and County School of Music.[60] Richter was clearly well-established in the musical community and in Leicester society.

In 1914 Richter was living in Germany. His father died in May. As well as sorting out his father's estate, Richter was conducting concerts and having treatment for his eyesight, which was becoming worse. When the War broke out the German authorities interned him at Ruhleben, as he was a British citizen. He was placed in secure accommodation, much like a prison. The conditions in these camps were quite poor. Worse still, he was subjected to the indignity of being treated like a criminal. Richter later claimed that he had been offered freedom by the German authorities if he renounced his British citizenship, but that he refused to do so.[61]

Richter returned to Britain in a prisoner exchange a month later, because he was too old to fight and had poor eyesight. Then in December 1916 a letter to a friend in Berlin raised the suspicion of British authorities. Sending the usual Christmas wishes, he fondly recalled evenings at their house, and finished with *"May God and his blessing be with you my dear friends and with all my countrymen."* [62] This was the sum total of Richter's expression of 'support' for the enemy. He may have been naïve, but he did not express any anti-British sentiment or desire that Germany should win the War. However, in the current climate of fear, this was enough for him to be considered dangerous.

In February 1917 he was arrested and interned under the Defence of the Realm regulations. A newspaper article reported at the time of his arrest that he *"has twice been prosecuted under the Lighting Restrictions Order for exposing a naked light."* [63] The Order was designed to guard against the threat of aerial bombardment.

Richter used his society connections to make the case for his release. Lady Warwick, using the influence of Lord Curzon, wrote to the Home Secretary, personally guaranteeing *"W. Richter's absolute loyalty to England all these years. To be interned for a month in Germany! & now interned here! is a scandal, isn't it?"* [64]

Another letter of support came from Mr. A. Mussell who was *"convinced that he is absolutely loyal to our country."* Mussell had known Richter for 20 years, and had been his pupil for the last five. He wrote that Richter fell out with his father because of *"his dislike of the domination of Prussian Militarism"*, which had only been *"strengthened by the present War"*.

Despite the efforts of his friends, Richter was interned in Islington, North London, at the end of February, 1917. It seems he was then transferred to a harsher camp, perhaps in response to the letter to his friend in Germany. In March his eyesight was bothering him, and he was trying to be transferred back to Islington for better care:

Why the street names were changed

"I beg protest against my imprisonment which I consider most unjust. I think in accordance with the supposed offence on my part internment is the extreme punishment that can be meated [sic] out to me, and I beg therefore that my readmission to Islington Camp where I have been quite happy you will kindly grant me." [65]

His doctor gave medical evidence confirming the trouble Richter had with his eyesight, adding that as *"a man of emotional temperament he has been rather depressed in spirits."* [66]

When Richter wrote to his lawyer, he asked him not to tell his wife, as *"it would break her heart"*. He also noted that he was only allowed to send one letter each month.[67] For an upstanding citizen like Richter, the shame of being treated as a criminal must have been very great.

In December 1917, Earl Grey was prevailed upon to write to the Home Office on Richter's behalf. Grey highlighted the fact that Richter was incapable of providing Germany with any assistance, adding: *"His only son has served in France, became very ill and was wounded, so returned after six months [in] hospital for Home Duty which he is now doing"*. He noted that *"Mr Richter has not one relation fighting on the other side."* [68]

Richter's son, Siegfried, had been fighting in the Royal Warwickshire Regiment.
This plea showed how powerful and unaccountable the British state was during the War, and how even the well-connected were powerless in its face. Richter had not been tried or convicted. The Home Secretary simply issued an order for him to be interned *"in the interests of public safety."* [69] Successive applications for Richter's release were made, but failed. The War provided justification for the government to intervene in the everyday lives of its citizens to an unprecedented degree.

Photographs of Willibald Richter from his expulsion papers in 1919

In August 1918 Richter applied to be denaturalised and released. He wrote: *"I now beg to inform you that in consequence of the treatment I have experienced at the hands of the British Government and also because my status as a British subject has not protected my liberty, I cannot consider myself as such any longer and herewith my British citizenship."* [70] This was refused,[71] but in October 1918 he appealed again. By December 1918 his citizenship had been fully revoked, and in March 1919 he was repatriated to Germany.[72]

Richter's wife, Charlotte, had moved to London in February 1917 and changed her name back to Rushworth. A German name would not have helped her to settle in Hampstead. With the exception of a brief meeting in 1920, she had been separated from her husband for almost a decade when, in 1924, she made a successful request for him to be allowed to return home.[73]

Why the street names were changed

MUSIC

▌ The Ride of the Valkyries halted

It was not only Herr Richter, a German musician, who was affected by the War. German music itself came under censorship. Before the War, German culture had been very popular in Britain. German music, literature and art were held in high regard. The music of Beethoven, Bach, and especially Wagner was played regularly at De Montfort Hall. *The Ride of the Valkyries* played on the magnificent organ was especially popular. However, soon after the outbreak of War, German music and musicians fell out of favour. By the end of 1914, English composers, especially of nostalgic and nationalist songs, had replaced Germans.

After the War, German music was quickly rehabilitated, and in 1925 Siegfried Wagner conducted the London Symphony Orchestra, playing some of his father's music as part of the prestigious international celebrity concert subscription series at De Montfort Hall. As the name suggests, people bought tickets for several concerts, and this brought musicians of international renown to the city. By this date, Siegfried Wagner could be celebrated and used to promote the event.

▌ The sinking of the Lusitania: Riots ensue

On 7th May 1915 The German navy sank the RMS *Lusitania*, killing 1,153 civilian passengers and crew, 128 of them American.[74] The boat was transporting a mixed cargo which included munitions, and some have suggested that the mixed cargo was part of a deliberate move to get the Germans to sink the ship, thus motivating the Americans to join the War.[75] This was a significant event in the growth of anti-German feeling. There was a huge outcry, and riots in many parts of Britain.[76]

In Leicester there is evidence of only one riot in response to the tragedy, aimed at someone who

German painting of RMS *Lusitania* sinking (Creative Commons)

was not actually German. The police were unable to control the crowd's fury against the alleged "'pro-German' tendencies…of Mr G.H. Leeson, pork butcher. King Richard's Road [was] the centre of an excited demonstration just after nine o'clock on Wednesday night and four windows were smashed."[77] Businesses which were actually owned by Germans suffered heavily in some areas. In Leicester, the younger son of Wildt & Co. fled to the United States, and a German delicatessen had to close.[78]

PATRIOTISM AND THE PRESS

Newspapers were the main source of information about the war. On the sinking of the *Lusitania*, *The Times* described "the hideous policy of indiscriminate brutality which has placed the German race outside of the pale. The only way to restore peace in the world, and to shatter the brutal menace, is to carry the war throughout the length and breadth of Germany. Unless Berlin is entered, all the blood which has been shed will have flowed in vain."[79] The Defence of the Realm Act ensured that only 'patriotic' articles were published, with the threat of prosecution for others. Recruiting posters reinforced the message of German brutality. The influence of these consistent messages would have been considerable.

Why the street names were changed

Soldiers marching in London Road (Record Office)

■ The soldiers return

"The cream of England slaughtered"

South Highfields residents would have witnessed large numbers of troops marching down London Road. They would also have seen many wounded soldiers being conveyed from the Midland Railway Station to the Fifth Northern General Hospital.

Hilda Stacey remembers:

"There were so many young families around us. One family, they were quite clever, Murphy's their name was, and they were all killed. Thousands were killed, the cream of England slaughtered. We used to go down London Road, and we saw the wounded soldiers coming in and we saw the soldiers going out. They used to march to the music. They were going to the coast to get on the ships to France...To us, it was another world."

Why the street names were changed

Nurse lights a cigarette (Record Office)

The base hospital, known as the Fifth Northern General Hospital, was set up in the old asylum on the edge of Victoria Park. It is now the Leicester University administration building.

James Allcock used to go and visit soldiers in the makeshift wards constructed for them:

"They had wards in corridors outside. We used to get through the railings and go onto these emergency wards, and fetch fish and chips for the soldiers. Well, us lads got caught by the sister one day, and she said 'If there's something you want to do, I'll give you something to do' and we finished up making swabs and rolling bandages. We enjoyed it. We used to go every night from school, doing it."

Hilda Stacey also used to visit the soldiers with her mother:

"Mother used to take us to see all the wounded soldiers. The university was the base hospital. The policemen there used to say 'If they're lonely, will you have them in the house, will you fetch them for tea?' And Mother did.

She was very good. No matter how poor you were, you always had something for somebody else."

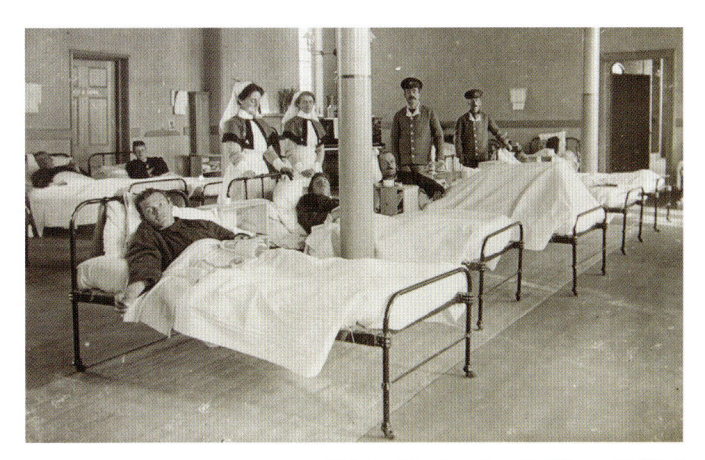

Wards at the base hospital (Record Office)

The sight of wounded soldiers being wheeled around the town centre must have fuelled rage at the Germans, who were perceived to be responsible.

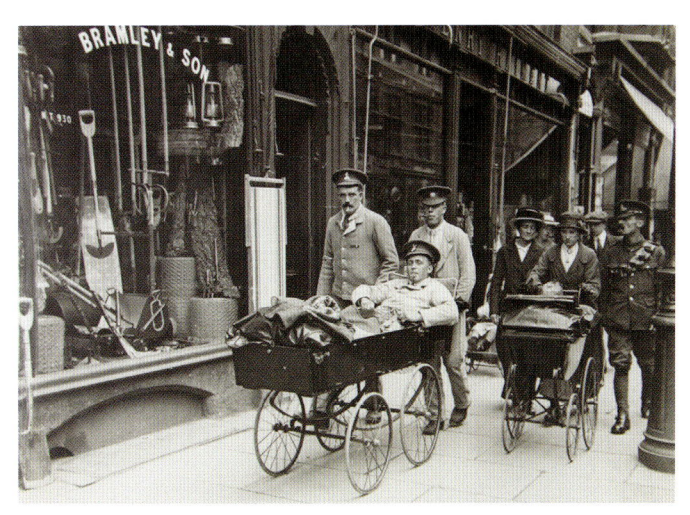

Wounded soldiers from the base hospital 1918 being pushed along Granby St. (Record Office)

45

Why the street names were changed

■ German names

For Germans living in Britain their names were, at best, an embarrassment. Many businesses suffered a loss of trade or broken windows if they even appeared to be German. George V changed the royal family's name from Saxe-Coburg and Gotha to Windsor in 1917. If they could, private citizens with German-sounding names followed suit, but it required the permission of the Home Secretary.[80] German people were subject to many controls. Some, as we have seen, were interned. Others were repatriated. A great deal of their property was confiscated by the British state.[81]

STREET NAMES

"to obliterate forever Hunnish names from our streets"

Queen Victoria and Prince Albert had been very popular monarchs. In South Highfields the names Gotha and Saxe Coburg had been given to two streets and to houses within them. There was also Hanover Street and Mecklenburg Street. Some other houses had been given German names as well.

Bismarck Villas:*	12-14, Mecklenburg Street
Saxe Coburg House:	2, Mecklenburg Street
Gotha House:*	24, Gotha Street
Saxe Coburg Villas:	35-43, Saxe Coburg Street
Dantzic House:*	23, College Street (Dantzic/Danzig was the German name for Gdańsk in modern Poland, which was then in Germany.)
* Houses with asterisks still exist and have these names on them	

Photographs Andrew Thirlby

46

Why the street names were changed

Mecklenburg Street (Record office)

Some of the people living on these streets were unhappy with the German names. In October 1917 Mr J. H. Marlow from Mecklenburg Street contacted the Highways and Sewerage Committee about the South Highfields names. Another letter was submitted in November 1917.

Discontent also showed itself in other areas of Leicester and was soon actioned. A letter was submitted to the Council on 30th November 1917 about Battenberg Avenue in Knighton. The Knighton proposal had the consent of all residents and property owners, and in January 1918 those living on Battenberg Avenue successfully had the name of their street changed to Carisbrooke Avenue. Battenberg referred to Prince Alexander Battenberg, Lord Carisbrooke, so the new name referred to the same person but no longer appeared to be German. Curiously, Battenberg Road, off Tudor Road, did not have its name changed.

The South Highfields name changes were delayed for two reasons. Firstly, Mr J. H. Marlow had approached the Council before having gained the necessary support from two thirds or more of people living in the street who paid rates - equivalent to today's Council Tax. Secondly, there was debate over the names, which was reflected in many letters to the press.

A letter to the *Mercury* from someone signing himself "Wounded Discharged" asked for help 'to wipe out those names which remind us of memories we are trying very hard to forget…to obliterate forever Hunnish names from our streets.' [82]

Mr. Wetherhead wrote in to suggest 'Ellis Road' as the new name for Mecklenberg Street. One correspondent suggested Saxe Coburg should be renamed Stratford "in memory of Shakespeare, who loved England". [83] A letter signed "Compadre" suggested that Portuguese names would be best to "perpetuate the memory of this small, brave nation who have sent their men to fight beside our own in the trenches." [84]

Reverend Cecil Robinson from Saxe Coburg Street went so far as to suggest what he called 'the Irish method' of bringing about change. "Most of your readers have probably realised it is quite useless to try and influence through the Press the little oligarchy who manage our local affairs. I do not wish to incite violence, but I imagine the Irish method of bringing English authorities to reason is the only one that would be at all productive."

However, some disagreed that change was needed. One correspondent, signed "Gotha Street", wrote "Shall we also boycott…the 'Messiah'…and the glorious music of Mozart because the composers were German, or shall we retain a little British Common Sense?" [85]

In April 1918 there was a petition from householders in Hanover, Saxe Coburg, Gotha and Mecklenburg Streets "requesting the Council to cancel the German names of those streets and substitute English names." At a full Council meeting, various opinions were expressed. Alderman Banton complained that changing names required "reason…not a passion." The Labour Party thought changing names "would not add to the dignity of the Council". [86] One Councillor suggested that "To call a street Gotham Street was to label the people living in it as people of weak mind." [87]

Why the street names were changed

For others, as Councillor J. K. Kelly put it, the matter was "too silly for words." [88] To these objections, the *Mercury* simply stated that "German names and German products are... anathema." [89]

On 29th October 1918 the Council approved changes to these street names in South Highfields. The following February, Bismarck Street in the West End was renamed Beaconsfield Road.[90] All these street names remain today.[91]

Here are the name changes to the South Highfields streets:

Old name	New name
Hanover Street	Andover Street
Saxe Coburg Street	Saxby Street
Gotha Street	Gotham Street
Mecklenburg Street	An extension of the existing Severn Street

Saxby street in 1915 ...

... and in 2014 (photograph Dipak Mistry)

Scale of Miles
200
300
400
500
MADE IN U.S.A.
HEBRIDES
C. Wrath
ORKNEY IS.
The Minch
Wick
Moray Firth
Inverness
SCOTLAND
Ben Nevis
Aberdeen
Perth
Dundee
Paisley
Glasgow
Edinburgh
Firth of Forth
North Channel
Quebec–Liverpool
IRELAND
Donegal Bay
Londonderry
NORTHERN IRELAND
Lough Neagh
Belfast
IRISH FREE STATE
SAORSTÁT EIREANN
Galway
Dublin
Limerick
Shannon R.
Killarney
Cork
Cobh
C. Clear
ISLE OF MAN
IRISH SEA
Barrow
Liverpool
Stoke-on-Trent
Birmingham
WALES
Swansea
Cardiff
Bristol Channel
Bristol
Lands End
SCILLY IS.
Plymouth
Southampton
Brighton
Portsmouth
Dover
Strait of Dover
London
Thames R.
Oxford
Leicester
Norwich
The Wash
Nottingham
Manchester
ENGLAND
Leeds
York
Hull
Humber
Gateshead
Newcastle
Sunderland
GREAT BRITAIN
NORTH SEA
Dogger Bank
Edinburgh–Copenhagen 620 m.
Hull–Copenhagen
London–Oslo 658 m.
London–Copenhagen
Hamburg–Buenos Aires 6619 m.
St. George's Channel
English Channel
London–Bordeaux 725 m.
Liverpool 3073 m.
2876 m.
Plymouth 3131 m.
Havre 3293 m.
London 3442 m.
Hamburg 3749 m.
CHANNEL IS. (Br.)
Cherbourg
USHANT
Brest
Rennes
BELLE ILE
Nantes
Angers
Loire
Tours
Le Mans
Orleans
Le Havre
Rouen
Seine R.
Amiens
Calais
Ostend
Bruges
Lille
Versailles
Paris
Marne R.
Oise R.
Reims
Luxembourg
FRANCE
Limoges
Clermont-Ferrand
Lyon
St. Etienne
Bordeaux
Garonne R.
Dordogne R.
Toulouse
Bayonne
Adour R.
Pic Nethou E. 11,168 Ft.
PYRENEES
ANDORRA
Montpellier
Nimes
CEVENNES
Avignon
Rhone R.
Marseille
Toulon
Nice
Cannes
Monaco
Grenoble
Dijon
Besançon
Mulhouse
ALSACE
Nancy
Metz
Strasbourg
Gulf of Lions
C. Creus
ATLANTIC OCEAN
Bay of Biscay
Lisbon–Bordeaux 733 m.
C. Ortegal
Gijon
Oviedo
Santander
Bilbao
San Sebastian
CANTABRIAN MTS.
Valladolid
Salamanca
SIERRA GUADARRAMA
Madrid
Toledo
Saragossa
Ebro R.
Segre R.
Barcelona
Tarragona
Valencia
Jucar R.
Guadiana
Guadalquivir R.
SIERRA MORENA
Seville
SPAIN
BALEARIC IS. (Sp.)
MINORCA
Palma
Gibraltar–Marseille
Genoa–Gibraltar 860 m.
Marseille–Port Said
CORSICA (Fr.)
C. Corso
Bastia
Ajaccio
Strait of Bonifacio
SARDINIA
Sassari
ELBA (It.)
NETHERLANDS
Zuider Zee
FRISIAN IS.
Groningen
The Hague
Amsterdam
Rotterdam
Antwerp
Ghent
Brussels
Liege
BELGIUM
LUXEMBURG
Rhine R.
Duisburg
Essen
Düsseldorf
Dortmund
Elberfeld
Cologne
Aix-la-Chapelle
Coblenz
Wiesbaden
Mainz
SAAR BASIN
Ludwigshafen
Mannheim
Karlsruhe
Stuttgart
Darmstadt
Frankfurt
Würzburg
Nuremberg
Augsburg
Munich
Danube
Lake Constance
Münster
Osnabrück
Hanover
Bremen
Weser R.
Ems R.
Wilhelmshaven
HELGOLAND (Ger.)
Hamburg
Altona
Lübeck
Kiel
Kiel Canal
Elbe R.
Brunswick
Magdeburg
Berlin
Potsdam
Stettin
Oder R.
Halle
Cassel
Erfurt
Leipzig
Dresden
Chemnitz
Plauen
ORE MTS.
Erzgebirge
GERMANY
Liegnitz
Görlitz
Breslau
Warta R.
Posen (Poznan)
Bromberg
RÜGEN
BORNHOLM (Den.)
DENMARK
Aalborg
Aarhus
Horsens
Odense
SLESVIG
ZEALAND
FALSTER
LAALAND
Copenhagen
Kattegat
The Sound
Skagerrack
The Naze
Bergen
Hardanger Fiord
Bukken Fiord
Stavanger
Oslo (Christiania)
Drammen
Siljan L.
Klar R.
Dal R.
Lake Wenner
Lake Wetter
Göteborg
Jönköping
Hälsingborg
Malmö
Karlskrona
London–Stockholm
Eger
Prague (Praha)
Pilsen (Plzn)
Bohemian Forest
Budějovice
Iglau
Brno
Olomouc
CZECHOSL
Linz
Vienna
Salzburg
Innsbruck
AUSTRIA
Klagenfurt
Grätz
TYROL
LIECHTENSTEIN
Basel
Zurich
Winterthur
Bern
Lucerne
Lausanne
Geneva
SWITZERLAND
Matterhorn 14,705 Ft.
Mt. Blanc E. 15,782 Ft.
ALPS
L. Maggiore
L. Como
L. Garda
Como
Turin
Milan
Verona
Venice
Padua
Alessandria
Genoa
Gulf of Genoa
Parma
Po R.
Modena
Bologna
Ravenna
SAN MARINO
Spezia
Lucca
Pisa
Florence
Leghorn (Livorno)
Ancona
Perugia
APENNINES
ITALY
Rome
Tiber R.
Naples
ADRIATIC SEA
Trieste
Fiume
Lyublyana (Laibach)
Zagreb (Agram)
Drava R.
Sava R.
Banaluka
Zara (It.)
YUGOS
(SERB-CROAT
Sarajevo
Cattaro (Kotor)
Lake Balaton
Bari
Pressburg (Bratislav)

PART TWO | GLOBAL IMPACT AND PEOPLE'S JOURNEYS

CHAPTER FOUR | The War in Europe

Over the past century, people of different communities from every corner of the globe have chosen to make South Highfields their home. In the second part of this book we hear some of their family histories. They all start with World War One and in so doing shed some light on the impact of the War on their country. For some this is because the War was fought on their soil, for others their country sent soldiers to fight, while some families had already made the journey to Britain. However detailed or sketchy the family memory of that long-ago time, they all tell us about particular issues for their country during the War.

World War Two followed on as a result of World War One as did many long journeys of migration, sometimes over several generations. These journeys help us understand something of the impact on individuals caught up in the global politics of war, of changing borders and of changing ideology, of colonialism. Those who are here now can tell us on behalf of those who did not survive. Through them we learn more about the uses of education and religion and we also learn about the challenges and processes of integration. They help us to understand how World War One shaped the face of our neighbourhood. We will hear stories from many places: from Europe and India, from Africa, the Caribbean and the Middle East. All reflect the devastating consequences of war.

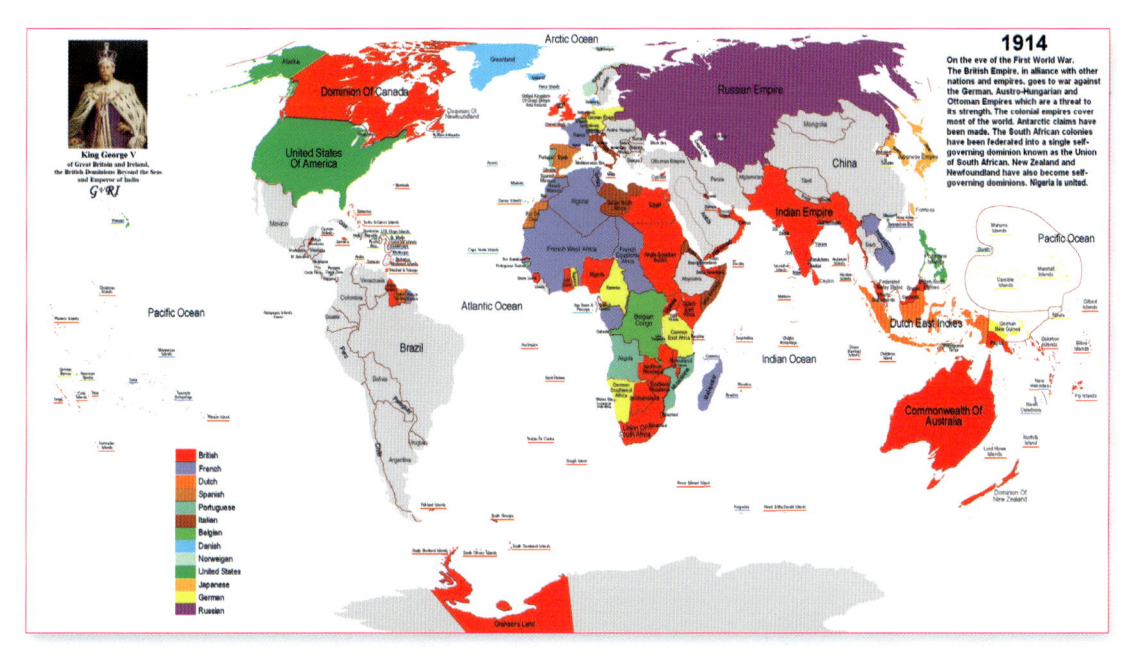

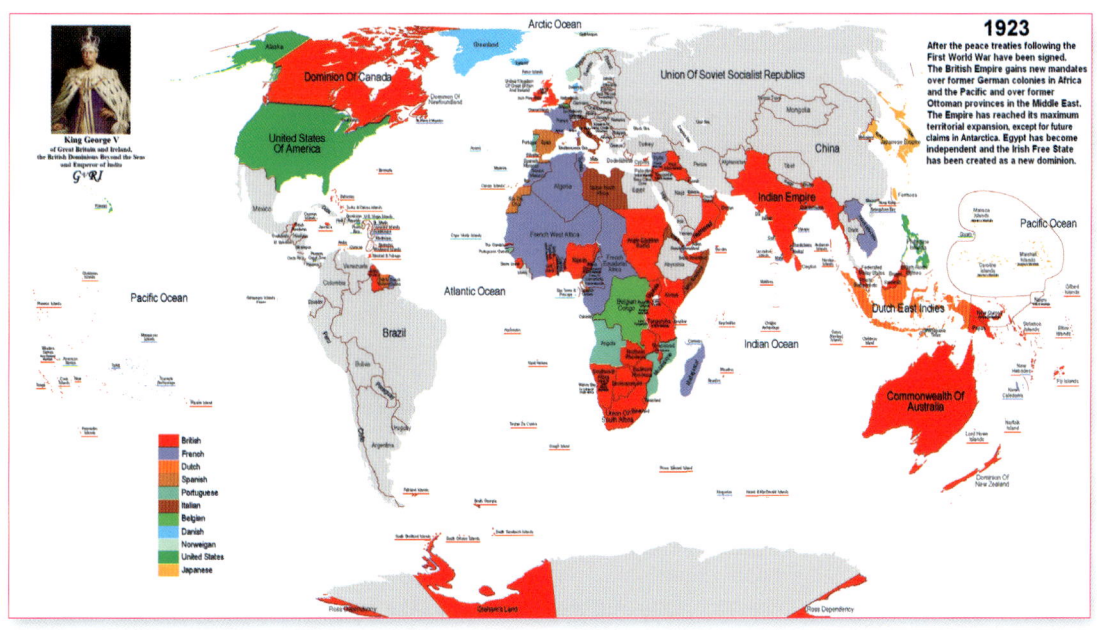

The War in Europe

1914
On the eve of the First World War. The British Empire, in alliance with other nations and empires, goes to war against the German, Austro-Hungarian and Ottoman Empires which are a threat to its strength. The colonial empires cover most of the world. Antarctic claims have been made. The South African colonies have been federated into a single self-governing dominion known as the Union of South Africa. New Zealand and Newfoundland have also become self-governing dominions. Nigeria is united.

1923
After the peace treaties following the First World War have been signed. The British Empire gains new mandates over former German colonies in Africa and the Pacific and over former Ottoman provinces in the Middle East. The Empire has reached its maximum territorial expansion, except for future claims in Antarctica. Egypt has become independent and the Irish Free State has been created as a new dominion.

Map of the world in 1914 and 1923

The War in Europe

The First World War started in Europe and all the major European powers were involved. Europe after 1919 was largely made up of nation-states. This chapter includes ten stories from Ireland, Poland, Turkey, Serbia, Czechoslovakia, Russia and Germany. It concludes with some German art from that time which is in the permanent German Expressionist Gallery at New Walk Museum. The fathers of four of the people who talked to us fought in WW1 whereas Piotr describes his grandparent's experience of the War. They lived in what was then Ukraine and part of the Austro-Hungarian Empire and later became Poland and then the Soviet Union and then Poland again. His grandparents did not move but the borders around them moved. Eastern Europe and Russia is mentioned in several stories in this chapter but we start over in the far west of Europe, in Ireland.

▌ Ireland

In the nineteenth century there were several uprisings in Ireland against British rule. In September 1914, the British government was ready to give Ireland some degree of independence called Home Rule. However in September of that year the decision was made to postpone it until the end of the War.[92] Many Catholics objected to having to wait longer for Home Rule, and wondered if it would ever happen. Sinn Féin, the Irish Republican Party, campaigned against enlisting. A higher proportion of Protestants, who were loyal to the Crown, enlisted than Catholics.

Nevertheless substantial numbers of soldiers did enlist from all parts of Ireland. Their experience is often overshadowed by the Easter Rising of 1916 when 450 people were killed and nearly 2,500 injured. The leaders were subsequently tried and executed. By the end of the War, most Catholics supported complete separation from Britain. An armed struggle for Irish independence would follow.[93]

Patrick Breen

"He was left in no man's land...for three days"

Pat has lived in Highfields all his life. His parents met in the Wolsey hosiery factory where his mother was an overlocker and his father, Peter Breen, was 'sweeping up'. His mother was a Protestant from Leeds and his father a Catholic from Bunclody, County Wexford in Ireland. Pat was their only child. His mother was 47 when he was born and his father was 67. He died in 1961 when Pat was 12. He had served in the Dublin Fusiliers.

Pat and his parents at Skegness

The War in Europe

"As a 12-year-old, I remember him walking with a stick. I actually remember him putting his leg on in the mornings, which seemed quite natural - but of course it's not - as a child. So he had this artificial leg, because he'd lost it just below the knee. He had 47 operations. He went to Roehampton, a limb hospital in London. He used to go every couple of years... He'd have perhaps a minor operation on his leg. I think he lost his leg in Mons...What I do remember is, he told me he went over the top of the trench. He got shot, as the people went forward. He was left in no man's land, and he was there for three days, as far as the story goes. A shell hit him. He saw that his foot was getting worse; in fact his foot was blown off. It was hanging there. It was getting onto the rest of his leg... He got a knife and he cut it off. He bandaged it the best way he could, because he was concerned about gangrene. In about three days, as I can remember him talking about it to other people in the pub, he was picked up and taken to hospital, but he must have had more of his leg amputated, because the amputation was down to below his knee, and that was because gangrene had started to spread. Then after the hospital he was discharged from the army, with this version of the wooden leg which they had then."

Pat is not sure why his father fought in the British Army.

"He was 32 in 1914, so if I'm right, he may have been over to England and gone back to Ireland, and joined up in Ireland...But at the start of the War there was an idea by some, by a chap called Redmond - this was the August time, I imagine - that if the War was over by Christmas, Ireland could have Home Rule. Him being Irish, and he was left-wing in his politics as well...and that's why he may have joined up. The paradox, the consequence of him being left-wing and yet fighting for what was then Great Britain, because Ireland was part of Great Britain. So he may well have joined up because he thought he was helping to free Ireland from the British."

Pat thinks it may have been poverty which drove his father into the army:

"He could well have been poor. It could have been regular food, clothes, and a lack of knowledge about the horrors, the reality of the war at that stage in 1914 – what it was actually like over there in Europe."

In the 1950s a lot of Irish people moved to Leicester and settled in Highfields. The pubs were useful meeting places for finding work and lodgings. People often stayed at Pat's house.

"It was a big house, a corner house on Bakewell Street. There were three rooms, which could be four rooms where people could live, and in fact they did at various stages, and the young Irish lads who stayed there for periods of time. I remember there was an Italian chap... and he had a disabled leg, as well. There were other people as well. There was a chap who worked at the Bell Hotel, which doesn't exist anymore. He was a waiter. The connection was in the pub, where he heard of people who needed somewhere to stay."

It was in the pub that Pat heard about his father's war experiences.

"I'd sit out the back of the Imperial, have crisps and pop and he'd talk...It was pretty gruesome. I don't think he could talk about it at home...He didn't like Winston Churchill at all, and the only time I ever heard him swear was in connection with Churchill's name. I think that was over the heavy bombing of Dresden towards the end of the Second World War. Of course, I wasn't born then, but I remember him talking about that... The main thing I remember him saying to me: 'Don't volunteer for anything.'"

The War in Europe

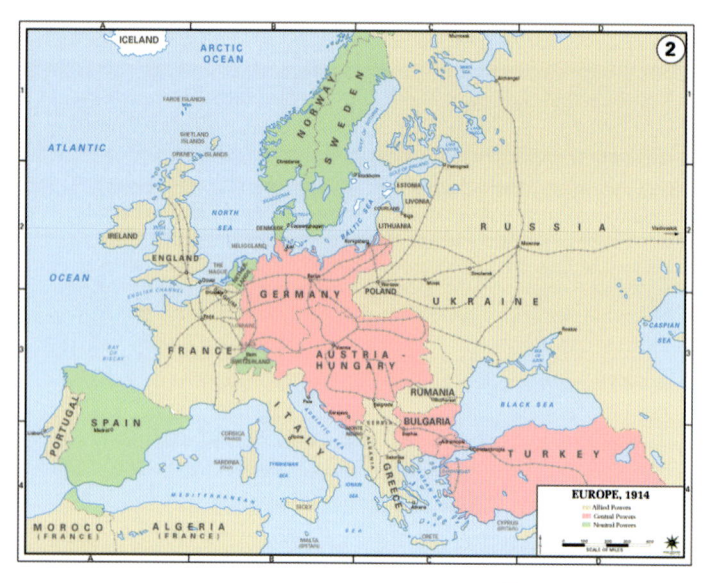

Map of Europe in 1914

▍Poland

Poland's decline in the 18th century led to its partition by Germany, the Austro-Hungarian Empire and Russia, so in 1914 it did not exist as an independent state. At the end of the War, Poland emerged again as an independent republic. Its changing boundaries are reflected in the story of Piotr's grandparents.

Piotr Kuhivchak

"According to the Soviet law, we were not considered the family."

Piotr was born in Poland and moved to Britain in 1985. He has lived in South Highfields since 1989.

"During the First World War my grandparents lived in the province of Galicia in what is now Ukraine, but at the time it was in the Austria-Hungarian Empire. And when the War broke out in 1914, as my grandfather was a subject of the Austria-Hungarian Empire, he was drafted into the army. So he went, and a lot was happening on the Eastern Front. The Germans made advances very quickly against the Russians. And there were several major battles in 1915/1916. My grandfather was injured in 1915, when the major Austria-Hungarian offensive was taking place. I know that he was injured in two places, in his leg and in his back. I understand, my father was telling me, it was the shrapnel. He was taken to hospital in Vienna, and he was very well treated medically, and got a very long stay in hospital and then a sanatorium. When he was discharged, he was not taken back into the Austria-Hungarian army so he went back home, and everything there was in a way like before, because he had a farm. However, the end of the First World War for that part of the world meant a lot more than for the West, because new countries were created. Because, apart from the conflict with the Russians and the Austria-Hungarians and the Germans, there started arising local independent movements.

Where my grandparents lived there were different local governments, which even printed their own currencies. They had cows, and they were selling milk, and my grandmother was getting money in one of these funny currencies, and nobody knew what happened to it… In the 1970's, when my father went to visit his parents, they were doing some work in the house and they lifted the floorboards, and there was this money stashed down there. My grandmother thought 'this was the new government, this is the money.' So she saved the money but it turned into nothing, because the next government came with the next currency."

However they had a good life, as his grandfather was given a generous War pension which was then honoured by the Polish government when their farm became part of Poland. He used the pension to buy land and expand the farm, and all was well until 1939 when the Soviets invaded and collectivised their land. They were given only a very small amount to live on. From then until they died in their 70s they were supported by Piotr's parents. They sent them food parcels, and when Piotr's father got permission to visit once every two years he was allowed to take them money.

The War in Europe

"They didn't move, but the Soviet Union moved in where they lived… we were not allowed to visit them and they were not allowed to come and visit us, because according to the Soviet law we were not considered the family: the family as they defined it. Only my father was the son of my grandparents, so he could travel."

Later in life, when Piotr's grandfather was swimming in a river one day, some shrapnel came out of his body. It had been lodged there since the First World War. Following the collapse of the Soviet Union in the 1990s, the Polish Government passed a law to compensate people like Piotr's grandparents who had suffered in this way. Most people by then had either died, or could not prove land ownership by their ancestors, but Piotr's brother was able to do so. Piotr used the compensation money to go to Poland. Four years ago, he and his wife Felicity went to visit the farm of the grandparents he had never met.

"I saw the house where they lived and the farm, but the farm was completely ruined. The Soviets had a planning system of what should grow where, but they didn't take into account local conditions like climate or soil. They cut down a huge orchard, as wheat had to be grown there. My grandfather must have felt awful. What all his life he had been working on, was gone into ruin. World War One for my father's family was strangely enough a positive experience. The Second World War was absolutely different; it was horrendous."

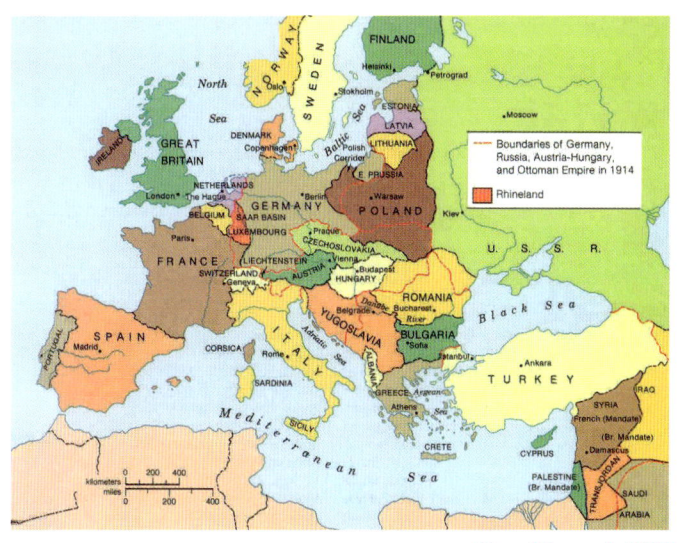

Map of Europe in 1923

Jozef Jundzill

"They opened the doors and said 'If there is anybody dead, get them out.'"

Jozef was born in 1934 in north-east Poland, in what is now Belarus. His father was born in the district of Vilnius which is now in Lithuania.

"My father Adolph Jundzill was born in 1898, and when he was 16 he was sent to Russia – let's say displaced from Poland – just before the War… His father was a specialist forester and he was sent to look after huge forests in Russia. He built churches and small wooden bridges, but his speciality was forestry… It was in Samara…My father got a job in a food processing factory… They stayed there throughout the War… In 1917 the Russian Revolution came, and then peace, and then they came back to Poland… He said it took three months with a cart and horse to travel to Poland."

The family then lived a settled life until the Second World War. Josef remembers the day when Russian

The War in Europe

soldiers came to their house in Luzhki, North East Poland in what is now Belarus. It was 10th February 1940:

"They knocked heavily on the door... with their rifle butts. My father opened the door. There was a Russian officer and two civilians...Then the Russian officer told my father to raise his hands and searched him... Then he said 'You have one hour to pack your things and you are going to be deported'...My father spoke perfect Russian...The officer was quite kind... We took clothes and eiderdowns, some food. He told my father to wring the chickens' necks and there was half a pig hanging in the pantry, he said 'grab that'...It was very cold. The snow was a metre high... We loaded it all onto a sledge driven by horse, and were taken to a gathering point in a school... It was still snowing... I was wrapped in the clothes and eiderdown on the sledge with my two sisters and my mother...then eventually early in the morning we reached the station and were loaded into the goods wagons...There was a stove in the middle with a tube going to the outside. There was a lower berth and higher berth...We had to wait for more people..and many more people eventually were packed into the wagon...There was a toilet: just a hole in the floor boards... with potato sacks hung up in the top... eventually when we were travelling the stove was lit... we were taken to north-east Russia. It took about three weeks. On the stations, they opened the doors and said 'If there is anybody dead, get them out. If there is anybody ill, help yourself to some hot water.'"

This was the first of many long journeys for Jozef. The family were sent to a labour camp in Russia, 500 miles north of Kotlas. His parents felled trees and prepared the ground for crops. In August 1941, the Polish people were freed from labour camps and prison camps and taken to communal farms in Kyrgyzstan following a pact between Russia and Poland to join together against the Germans. The men joined the army and were trained as the Polish army in exile. There were 70,000 men, but the Soviets could not provide the food and weapons needed. Many men died of typhoid, hunger, lice and exhaustion.

Joe and his mother before the war

On the way to Krygyzstan they lost Jozef's father when he went off to look for food while the train was in a station. Jozef, his mother and sisters survived by living on a bag of onions. Conditions were hard in the camp in Kyrgyzstan. They needed proof that Jozef's father was in the military, in order to get help and information from the Polish office in town. They had no proof, but were helped by a kind young soldier who lied, saying he knew Jozef's father.

The War in Europe

In August 1942 they were told they could leave, and they were taken by train, boat and lorry to Tehran. The Polish soldiers had been handed over to the British to be retrained. Stalin agreed that the British could also take civilians, as the Soviet Union had little food to feed them.

"From Tehran we were taken...in passenger trains... The English army were also travelling with us. The transport manager, a Polish chap, asked for someone to look after the last wagon with pencils and books for schools...and my mother said 'I will'... and I enjoyed travelling with sacks of books...in that goods wagon... we met English soldiers...I remember hot, sweet tea with condensed milk...my first taste of English tea in big containers waiting for us in the stations".

They were then taken to Ahvaz in Iran where, in 1943, Jozef and his mother and sisters were visited by their father for the first time. By that time he was with the army in what is now Iraq, and soldiers were allowed to see their families. From there his father was taken to Egypt, and at the end of 1943 was sent to Britain. He joined the Polish RAF as a butcher in catering, having been trained in food processing in Russia during World War One. He was a chef at the Polish officers' mess in Lincolnshire Bomber Command and he stayed there throughout the war.

Meanwhile Jozef's mother was given the choice by the British of going to Africa or India, and she chose India. They were taken with 5,000 others to Karachi and after several months to Valivade near Kohlapur in India, where they stayed until partition in 1947. It was a happy time for Jozef with lots to do, including the boy scouts.

"We thought we would go back to Poland, but since Poland had been communised and was ruled by Russia, the Polish army said they didn't want to go back to Poland. Bevin gave us a choice: 'You can go to England or Argentina or Australia.' My father decided to stay in England. The army was disbanded; soldiers retrained.

Joe and his father at a similar age (Joe on the left)

Father stayed in catering, and when we came to England, we got together."

They were taken to an RAF camp in Melton Mowbray. Jozef found it strange.

"It was damp and cold after India. It affected my mother more than me. I remember I went to town in scout uniform, and in Woolworths everybody was looking at me as if I was weird. It was November, but I was very tanned and in short trousers."

Jozef went to college and in 1952 found work in Leicester, where he has lived ever since. His parents' marriage did not survive the many separations. Jozef's own marriage was brief.

"I got married and we didn't have children. I married in '75, and in 1980 was a free man again."

The War in Europe

Joe in 2014

This is an extract from a long talk with Jozef. He is a man with many stories and vivid memories. He lives locally, and goes regularly to the lunch club at St. Peter's Community Centre.

▮ Turkey

In 1914, the Ottoman Empire covered a vast area. It included what is now Turkey, together with the whole of modern Iraq, Israel, Jordan, Kuwait, Lebanon, Palestine, Syria and most of modern Saudi Arabia. After World War One, modern Turkey emerged from the Ottoman Empire. Britain and France took control of most of the remaining area.

Mehmet Aydin

"They realised there were Muslim soldiers opposite… they were fighting Muslims."

Mehmet Aydin is from Turkey. He runs a thriving shop on St. Peter's Road and a busy restaurant on Highfield Street. His grandfather was killed at Gallipoli.

"My grandfather was in Gallipoli in 1916. He was in the military four and a half years, as at that time military service in Turkey was four and a half years. It was the Ottoman Empire before the republic of Turkey. He fought in Gallipoli. We heard from his colleagues and his friends that they used to fight close with the Anzacs, and in the daytime they would throw each other cigarettes, like friendly. They mentioned that inside the British army they heard that there were some Muslim prayers. They heard that they were reading the Koran. They realised there were Muslim soldiers opposite and they were fighting Muslims… There were rumours about this. There were a lot of casualties. Nearly 200,000 people died in that war. He was one of them, unfortunately."

Mehmet has visited Gallipoli:

"When you go to where the War took place, Gallipoli peninsula, there are some graveyards of dead soldiers: Anzacs, Australians, New Zealanders or English. They have their own cemetery. I visited there once. When you go there, you can feel the history. After the War

The War in Europe

the families of those who were buried there came to visit the cemetery…The founder of the republic of Turkey, Kemal Ataturk, said to the families 'They are our children, like they are your children. We will look after them, as you look after them.'"

Mehmet's father was six years old when his own father was killed. He was called up in 1930, by which time military service had been reduced to two and a half years. He was also in Gallipoli, working as a carpenter in the military. Mehmet's father did not have to fight in the Second World War, when Turkey remained neutral.

Mehmet came to Britain in 1990 when he was 22, to study at the University of North London Business School. Because he was not living in Turkey he only had to do 21 days' National Service and pay 6,000 Euros to the Turkish government. He has now lived in Britain for longer than he lived in Turkey.

"I go back every year to see my brothers and sisters, auntie, uncle … Two years ago I went for two weeks, and after nine or ten days I said 'What am I doing here? I don't belong here.' I felt like that. I wanted to come back here immediately".

Serbia

Serbia was involved in the First World War from the beginning. The assassination of Austria's Archduke Franz Ferdinand in Sarajevo was the immediate trigger for the conflict.

Archduke Franz Ferdinand with his wife Sophie, Duchess of Hohenberg, and their three children (from left), Prince Ernst von Hohenberg, Princess Sophie, and Maximilian, Duke of Hohenburg, in 1910 (Creative Commons)

The War in Europe

Ilija Preocanin

"England did not want any immigrants after World War One."

Ilija Preocanin is Serbian. He was born in 1928 and has lived in England since 1947. He is the president of the Serbian Chetnik Club on Saxby Street. Ilija's father served in the Serbian navy during the First World War.

"He spent some time visiting Newcastle and other ports in England and France, taking coal wherever it was needed for the other places and ships."

His uncle was killed during the War.

"When the War finished, a lot of them emigrated to America, Australia and other places…They realised they would have a better life, because Serbia had been ravaged by the War, the terrible War…England did not want any immigrants after World War One."

After the War Ilija's father continued to farm until he died in the 1970s. Ilija left his place of birth in 1944 with 15,000 other Chetniks (royalists) to avoid being captured by the Partisans (Communists) and fled to Slovenia, where he stayed until 1945. When the allies liberated Italy, they went there and lived in a refugee camp.

"Food was very poor, but we still managed to have a school and I managed to study English and Italian. There were a lot of qualified teachers there."

In 1947 they were transferred from Italy to Germany and were asked by the English, American and French authorities if they would like to return to Yugoslavia. They were also given the choice of working in England, Australia, France, America or Canada, where labour was needed.

Ilija chose England and arrived with another 8,000 Chetniks in late 1947. They were initially accommodated in army camps, and taken to farms and mines to work. Ilija came to Leicester in 1948 and used his knowledge of English to help others settle. He married his German wife in 1955. The club has been running in Saxby Street since the late 1960s. Ilija says there are about 500 Serbian households in Leicester now, but their children are:

"growing more in the English ways than in the Serbian ways…It is natural".

■ Czechoslovakia

The Austro-Hungarian Empire was made up of many different cultural and ethnic groups. After its defeat in the First World War, it was replaced by several nation states including Czechoslovakia, which included Czech and Slovak lands.

Alice Klaus

"my life was saved by a fortnight"

Alice was born in 1919 in Prague. Her father, Otto Klaus, was born in 1890.

"My father was born in Prague…He qualified as a medical doctor at the beginning of the First World War, and as a doctor he was recruited into the Austrian army, because Bohemia was at the time part of the Austrian empire. His War service was in Poland."

While he was in the army in Poland he met Mira, Alice's mother, and they married in 1917. Alice does not know much about her father's life in the army, but the subsequent family story flows from World War One.

"He emerged from this as very much against the War. Against wars. He had a brother who was fighting on the Russian front, who had been killed…it wasn't sure

The War in Europe

whether he was dead or taken prisoner. He went to that place where the War had taken place, and dug, and found his body. So it must have been a very frightening, very traumatic experience. He was one of four brothers. He was the eldest. All of them went to Prague University. And two of them did not survive the First World War. One died in battle against the Russians, and the other one contracted tuberculosis and died after the War. And the youngest actually became a refugee, and came to England and survived. But that is many years later."

Alice and her parents in about 1924

When the War ended, Otto and Mira moved to Prague, which was then in the newly-created Czechoslovakia, and Otto became a medical officer of health working mainly in Sudetenland, then a German speaking part of Czechoslovakia.

"My father came back as a socialist and that had an important influence on my upbringing, because right from an early age I used to go to meetings - the workers' meetings, family meetings - and I became very conscious of the fact that some people have a much more difficult life than others. In fact, it had some influence on my coming to England because, as a result of my contact with the socialist party, I made contact with the Woodcraft Folk. They had come from England to Czechoslovakia, to tell us what they were doing. And this played a very important part in my coming to England in the end, because they helped me to come, and I spent a long time with a Woodcraft family in London in 1938."

While Alice was in London she found out about the shortage of nurses and on return applied for and was granted a place at Southampton Children's Hospital. She left Czechoslovakia after the Munich crisis. Within two weeks of her arrival in England, the Nazis occupied Czechoslovakia. Alice then tried to get her parents to come to England.

"My life was saved by a fortnight. [Britain had] a Conservative government, and they were very much against accepting refugees. They preferred to accept people who were very rich. But, of course, we weren't very rich. I tried very hard [to get them over]. I was working as a nurse. They preferred to bring people over who could do manual work... I could already write English quite well. I worked in a children's hospital in Southampton. I worked there until Dunkirk. And [then] the government felt they didn't want to have any foreigners by the coast."

Her father hoped they would be safe in Czechoslovakia because of their age, his usefulness as a doctor and his service in the army during World War One.

The War in Europe

Alice on the balcony of the hospital in the summer of 1939

"And so they stayed. I had a brother who was five years younger, and, very sadly, he stayed as well. I did manage, in the very end, to arrange for him to come, but he was supposed to come more or less the week the War started."

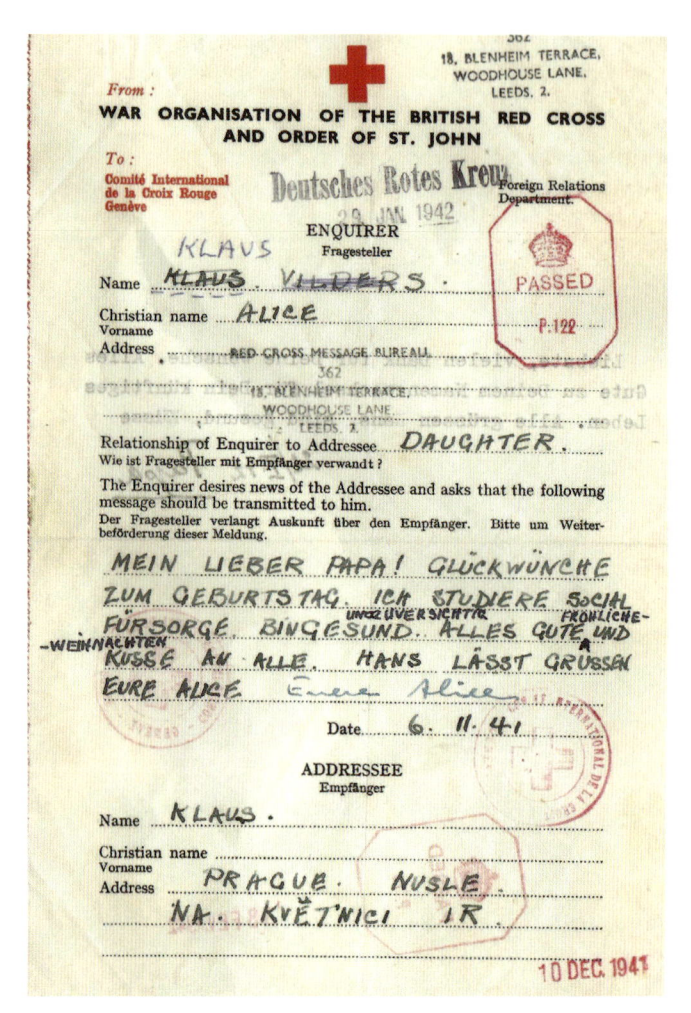

Alice sent this Red Cross message to her father on 6th November 1941. It reads: message "(Mein Lieber Papa!) My dear father! Happy Birthday. I am studying social care. Am healthy and optimistic. All the best, merry Christmas and kisses to everyone. Hans sends (his) regards. Your Alice" (then your Alice repeated with different spelling of your). The reply from her father read "Darling, many thanks for your well wishes. Congratulations on the name change for your future life. Everyone sends their best to Hans, are healthy, kisses. Papa."

The War in Europe

They were Jewish. In 1942 Otto, Mira and their son were taken to a local ghetto and in October 1944 they were:

"transported to Auschwitz, an extermination camp, from which they did not return".

Alice went on to qualify as a psychiatric social worker and worked in Highfields for many years until her retirement in 1988.

Alice in 2014

"After I retired, I worked for the university at Vaughan College, and I had students who were coming from all parts of the... professions to work on aspects of child abuse. I only retired from there round about 2000. And then we started the charity... I got interested in children who were very shy, who don't speak at school, who speak at home, but don't speak at school. Because these children were not being given a lot of help...We started a charity, a kind of parents' support group. This is the kind of work that I have done over the years, supporting parents who had... different kinds of problems. This book is helping parents:' Tackling Selective Mutism: A guide for professionals and parents'. And I've edited it, together with a speech and language therapist. "

Alice was awarded an OBE in 2011. She has two sons and five grandchildren. Her latest book was published in September 2014. [94]

▌ Russia

The vast Russian Empire extended from Poland to the Pacific. In 1914, together with Britain and France, it entered the War against Germany and the Austro-Hungarian Empire. The outbreak of the Russian Revolution in 1917 led to Russia's withdrawal from the War and the establishment of the Soviet Union, which lasted until 1991.

Felicity Kuhivchak

"My grandmother had to register with the police as an alien."

Felicity has lived in South Highfields since 1989 with her husband, Piotr. Although she was born in this country, her father's family were originally from Russia. Her history and current work shed useful light on migration, which is so much a feature of life in our area.

The War in Europe

"My father's family came over as Rosensteins from Lodz in what was then Russia and in 1918 became Poland. They came over in the 1890s as a result of the pogroms against Jews in Russia and the...tremendous over-population in that part of the Russian Empire. Russia was hostile to Jews all through the nineteenth century...Jews had been forbidden to own land, and generally to become part of the fabric of society. They were treated as outsiders on religious grounds, and because Russia hadn't developed a strong economic base...the Russian Empire hadn't found the use for Jews as middle men and financiers that had been found in more advanced countries...Kings had been on very good terms with rich Jews because the Jews were a kind of early banking system, and therefore could acquire quite a lot of power and secure some civic rights in other countries, but this wasn't yet the case in Russia. So my grandparents were part of an enormous wave of Jewish emigration which mostly went to America. They are the 'huddled masses' of the 1870s and 1880s who end up in Manhattan and Brooklyn. The Jews in Russia had to live 'beyond the pale'. I don't think it was a visible marker, but it was the zone where they were kept separate from the rest of the Russian Empire, and that's eventually why they were found there by the Germans when they invaded the Soviet Union. The reason there were so many Jews in Eastern Europe that the Germans felt they had to deal with, was that they were still inhabiting those towns and villages, the so-called shtetls of Jewish life, which now have no Jewish life in them at all, which were once substantially or wholly Jewish. Those towns were the towns which the Germans emptied during the Second World War."

Felicity's grandparents arrived as children and later met and married. They lived in the East End of London on Commercial Road above a shop, and lived an orthodox Jewish lifestyle. Felicity's father was born in 1919.

"My grandfather worked in the rag trade as a presser and my grandmother, I think, was just a housewife, although she had worked in a toffee factory from the age of eight. So she was child labour. They were not literate and spoke Yiddish at home. So the great problem for that family was how the children would manage an English education while coming home to a totally orthodox environment. As a result of the stress that set up, the eldest son became ultra-orthodox and ended up as the headmaster of a Jewish boys' school. All the other children broke away from the religion and married out of the religion."

Felicity is unsure why her grandfather did not fight in the First World War:

"Maybe he wasn't healthy enough, because he had a bad heart. Certainly the story in the family is that he suffered from the steam and heat of the workshops, and that he always had a very short temper and wasn't a well man".

Felicity's father served in the Second World War.

"My grandmother had to register with the police as an alien, and every time she went in she told them how many of her sons were fighting in the forces at that moment, and was very sharp with them about the injustice of being treated as an enemy alien...They changed their name in the Second World War and became Rosslyn after Rosenstein."

While he was recovering in hospital after wounds sustained in the Second World War Felicity's father met her mother, who was a nurse.

"They would never have encountered each other: a Jewish London family and a family from a village in Northamptonshire."

Interestingly, her mother's parents had also met through war when her grandfather, wounded at Passchendaele, was recovering in hospital and was visited by a choir of young women from Banbury, one of whom he later married. Her maternal grandfather

The War in Europe

"was drawn into the First World War as somebody who could work with horses, because his father had a pony and trap business, taking parcels to Northampton for the villagers... So he was taken into a cavalry regiment and managed the horses in the trenches."

"It was always very significant to my sister and me that we had this very mixed origin, that my father's family could see as far east as Russia, and my mother's family knew about the land and the farm, and a world that hadn't changed for centuries."

"Because I was interested in Eastern Europe and at school my comprehensive had taught Russian...as a second language, my sister and I both studied Russian for five years, and she went on to become a professor of Russian. I remembered enough Russian to be interested in Eastern European literature. I was working on a Polish female poet in the 1980s when I had the chance to go to Warsaw University for a study semester and Piotr was at the English department there."

Piotr later came to work at Warwick University and they married.

"I suppose this is a story about generations of Eastern Europeans finding a welcome here, and work, and a context in which they could flourish without having to give up any part of their life that was too precious to them. I think there is something about the porousness of English society which means that people can imagine a life here. It's worth it to give up what they are most familiar with, because there is opportunity here. I think there are two kinds of opportunity. One is what my grandfather found, of businesses which are run on very harsh principles, almost out of sight, in workshops where you're often kept on a very short lead by your own countrymen, or by people who know how to exploit you as immigrant....which still happens. But your children get free of that. One generation has a lot to put up with, then the next generation steps free of it. The other kind of immigration is intellectual immigration, like Piotr's, where his sense of his subject, and what he could do, is easier to fulfil in a country like this where there's already been a lot of immigration, a lot of absorption of other cultures,"

Felicity works as a family counsellor.

"One of the things I hear a lot in counselling now is mixed marriages, where it's the dramatic contrasts. They are hugely attracted by the 'otherness' of that person, because that is one of the great sources, I think, of attraction: that somebody doesn't remind you of anybody you grew up with. They represent danger and possibility and thrill, and they're real. According to the standards you were brought up with they shouldn't be real; they shouldn't exist. Here they are. And that can turn into a tremendous passion."

She also sees the adjustments of second and third generation migrants.

"You can't keep a child out of modernity except by blindfolding it and stopping its ears, and keeping its hands off the keyboard of every computer in the land. The information comes in, so whether you're trying to be ultra-Muslim or ultra-Hindu, or ultra-Jewish or evangelically Christian, you can teach a child that that stuff is bad, but you can't stop the information from flooding in. As the child develops its own ability to think, it will come to its own conclusion."

▚ Germany

Some Germans lived in Leicester during the War and others moved here later. Most people in Britain blamed the War on Germany and Austria, but the reality was much more complex, although Germany made the first hostile move in 1914 against Belgium and France. Life was also hard for ordinary people living and working in Germany, and their patriotism was just as sincerely felt. We have spoken to three people of German ancestry. Each of their stories highlights the movement of people around Europe and shows how their allegiances during the First World War were, for most,

The War in Europe

an accident of birth. Angela's parents were émigrés; Werner Menski moved to South Highfields in 1975; Alexander Kazmierz moved to Leicester six years ago. His great-grandparents fought on different sides.

Angela Walker

"windows were broken in the shop...there were anti-German riots"

Angela was born in England but has German ancestry. She has lived in Leicester for 30 years.

"On my father's side, my grandfather and my grandmother were both German émigrés. They lived in North London. Their parents had come over, I believe, in the 1860s. My great-grandfather was a tailor on my grandfather's side and on my grandmother's side my great-grandfather was a baker. They lived in Finsbury Park, Highgate area. That's where my Dad was brought up."

"My grandfather was involved in the First World War as a medic, a hospital orderly or porter or nurse, I'm not quite sure what he did. He wasn't a doctor. He was born in 1872, so by World War One he was already 42. And he'd been in the Royal Army Medical Corps since 1898. He joined the war as Sergeant Major Henry Bangert. Before the War he was stationed in Dublin and his family lived in barracks in Phoenix Park. Before that he was in South Africa. He went in 1900, which was in the middle of the Boer War. He stayed there until 1910. During that time his four boys were born. My grandmother was over there with him. They were married in 1904...in London. She went back out there and had William in 1906, Harry, who's my Dad, in 1907, Ted in 1910, and Johnny in 1913; and there was a daughter born after World War One."

"I believe my grandmother went back home to Finsbury Park to where her parents lived... That's where my grandfather came home on leave. They were bakers. I don't think they lived above the shop. There is a family story that their baker shop windows, which would probably have the name BEKKER over it: German name for baker. That was their family name. I have heard that the windows were broken in the shop, and I know that there were anti-German riots and other German tradespeople had the windows of their shops broken."

"My grandfather kept a diary, every day from the thirteenth of August when he embarked for France from Dublin until he actually left the Army, just before the Battle of the Somme in February 1916. So he wrote almost every day, apart from the period he went home on leave over the first Christmas 1914."

Sergeant Major Henry Bangert

"I'm writing this up as a blog and finding out a lot about him that way. He wrote about military campaigns going around him and he wrote about

The War in Europe

working in field hospitals. But he also wrote about all sorts of personal things, like letters he'd received from home. He talked about going for walks… meeting with French people, how friendly they seemed at first, and of the long, long marches he did in the beginning of the War - particularly towards Mons - and then they had to retreat back before they started digging trenches. He left the army suddenly. At the back of the diary, somebody has handwritten that he left because he had rheumatoid arthritis."

Angela's grandfather then worked in his wife's family bakery business. Angela's father worked as a baker too, until he decided to study divinity in his 20s. He became a curate in Norfolk. He was not brought up to speak German at home.

"When I was a child it was made quite clear to me that I was part German, and that was important, but I was also part Irish on my mother's side. So I never thought of myself as English to the core."

Angela found a very different German legacy when she went on a teaching exchange to Iowa in the United States. She stayed with a family who had arrived at about the same time in the 1860s and had left Germany for similar reasons - because of conscription and economic depression. However, they had kept their German language and identity, as had most of the German people in Iowa.

Angela concludes:

"I teach people who have come from all parts of the world in Leicester. My past makes me think very much of the shifting nature of our population, how Leicester has changed so much and Britain has changed so much. Where would we be without the people who had come from other places?"

Werner Menski

"Our entire family was affected by World War One"

Werner lived in Bochum in central Germany. In 1975 he moved to South Highfields into a building which used to be a Polish butcher's shop. He lived there until 2005 and still has connections with the area, as his wife runs the Centre for Indian Classical Dance which is based in Churchill Street.

"My father's family came from a part of Eastern Prussia that is today Poland and our entire family was affected by World War One: thrown all over Germany. I never knew my paternal grandmother who was overrun by Russians on the trek and later died, probably of starvation and/or typhoid. Coming from a part of the world that was directly affected by national boundary changes and invasions in World Wars One and Two, I have been reading a lot recently about what happened in 1944/45 in Eastern Prussia. The memory that people in that area had of the Russian invasion during World War One made them think, foolishly, that their treatment would not be as cruel as it turned out to be. Hence they did not leave in time and were overrun by the Russians, but they also were not allowed to leave, because fleeing was treated as treason."

Alexander Kazmierz

"you could get anything for alcohol or cigarettes. It was better than money"

Alex was born in 1975 in Heidelberg in Germany, and has lived in Leicester for six years. His great-grandparents fought on different sides in World War One.

"On my mother's side they came from Karlsruhe, Heidelberg and fought on the Prussian side for the Germans. My father's side came from the Russian side

The War in Europe

and fought for the Russians against the Austrians. In Crimea, I think, but I'm not sure about that. He fought until the revolution started. My father's side of the family is Jewish. It was odd, being Jewish and a soldier. It was the first war Jewish people actually were able to fight. He fled the Russian Empire to Switzerland because of the revolution in 1917, and then he resettled after the war in Germany - two different sides of the War - he met my grandmother and they married. So he married a German. It wasn't uncommon in that time to marry not Jewish. She was Protestant: Lutheran. Northern Germany was very Protestant, whereas Bavaria was very Catholic. It depends where you live, what your religion is. You used to swap (your religion) with your King. If your King was Catholic you became Catholic. If he was a Protestant, you had to become Protestant"

"On my mother's side they lived always in the German Empire near Baden on the French border, not far from Strasbourg. There was a fear that the War would come into Germany, but it never happened. It was so close to the front with France, and if it came into Germany it would have been a disaster for them."

As in other countries, people expected that the War would be over quickly. Life became difficult for soldiers and civilians. The winter of 1916 was very harsh and there was widespread hunger and cold, due to lack of food and coal. At the same time, naval blockades prevented ships delivering supplies to Germany.[95] An early frost killed off much of the potato crop. Many miners and farm workers had been called to fight. It became known as steckrübenwinter - "turnip winter" - as turnips became the staple diet.

"Nobody in my family died, as far as I know. It was easier because we grew up in the countryside. It was worse in the cities. Some farmers would sell on the black market, illegally. They made big money, especially in the major cities. My grandfather told me you could get anything for alcohol or cigarettes. It was better than money to exchange for basic foods."

Alex was asked if Germany is also commemorating the War, as we are in Britain:

"You get taught in schools about World War One and World War Two; it is more World War Two. We don't celebrate wars as you do in Britain. We have remembrance in Germany, but what is good in Britain is that everybody is proud of soldiers. But in Germany, as a soldier going in uniform through the streets, you can get assaulted. There is a very strong left-wing movement against war in Germany. They are against war. We remember the fallen, and every village has some remembrance in its graveyards: a little monument or something. Every church has the names of the fallen, the same like here. But as Germans we try to be not so remembered, because we always fear we may be responsible for starting World War One and especially World War Two, and the whole crime that was with World War Two."

Alex works in a very public role as a city warden. Has he had any problems?

"Because of my accent I have often been asked where I am from, and I say 'Germany' and people don't understand that somebody wants to live in Britain who is not from a poorer country, and I have to explain I am not here because of the money. I don't want to send money home. I am here because I have an English partner, I make my living here, I feel at home here. I have no problems being German. In fact the opposite is true - people say the German cars are the best. The 1966 World Cup: I have to listen to that a few times! But it is more of a joke. The royal family is a German family. I know Prince Charles's cousin lives in Germany."

The War in Europe

German Art

As in every country, there were people in Germany who opposed the war. Artists known as the German Expressionists were one such group. These two lithographs by Max Slevogt depict the horror of death both on the battlefield and at home. Max Slevogt (1868-1932) was commissioned as a War artist but he was then censored and condemned by the German Government when he produced such anti-war pieces. Among German artists at that time there was initial support for the War, as it appeared to offer a quick and essential cleansing of the old order, but as growing numbers were killed, this support soon gave way to horror and disgust.

Shellfire .Max Slevogt (Lithograph, 1917) New Walk Museum

There is a dark humour in this picture, as skeleton-like figures ride artillery shells as they fly towards enemy lines.

The Suicide Machine ironically criticizes the mechanised slaughter of the First World War. Civilians walking along a boulevard insert a coin, press a button, and are shot dead. Social class is of no concern: a well-dressed man has already met his fate, whilst another in a trench-coat approaches his.

The Suicide Machine. Max Slevogt (Lithograph, 1917) New Walk Museum

The originals can be found in the permanent exhibition at New Walk Museum, and are part of Leicester's renowned collection of early twentieth-century German art, which was begun in 1944 by Trevor Thomas. Thanks to the museum for permission to use them.

CHAPTER FIVE | The Wider World

The conflict spread very quickly around the globe. One of the main reasons was the size of European empires, especially the British Empire. Its colonies including India, parts of Africa and the 'White Settler' Dominions of Australia, Canada, and New Zealand. The colonies swiftly provided large numbers of troops. 1,500,000 soldiers were recruited from India alone, and 1,300,000 from the Dominions. [96]

In return, the colonies expected that Britain might grant them greater power and freedom. Many of the colonial troops serving in Europe became aware of the racism with which they were treated. They asked why they fought and died for the freedoms which they themselves were denied. In many places this led to the growth of nationalist movements which, by the end of the Second World War, began to put real pressure on the imperial powers. As Germany lost the War, its colonies in Africa were taken over by Britain, France, Belgium and South Africa. As the Ottoman Empire collapsed, France and Britain took parts of the Middle East which gave Britain access to the Iraqi oil fields.

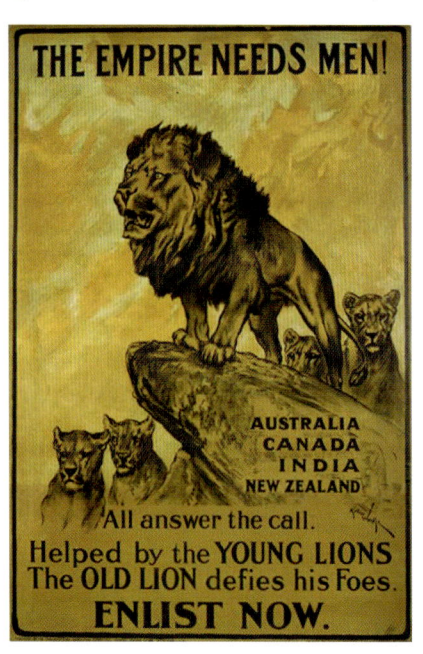

India

India was often described as the "jewel in the crown" of the British Empire. It was colonised by the British East India Company, which gradually took over the administration of individual provinces to secure trading rights. In 1857 the British Crown took over India and it became a formal colony run by the state, rather than a private company.

British colonies were required to provide soldiers for the War. Men were forcibly enlisted if there were not enough volunteers. Indian soldiers were one of the largest groups contributing to the forces during the First World War. Of the one and a half million men who were mobilised, 580,000 were combat troops. Brighton Pavilion was used as a hospital for injured Indian soldiers, with separate kitchens and accommodation for men from different religious groups and castes. Indian troops fought across the world, including Africa, the Western Front and the remains of the Ottoman Empire. The Punjab contributed disproportionately, so that there were many Sikhs, as well as Hindus and Muslims, who fought in the War[97] Many young men died a very long way from home.

Surinderpal Singh Rai

"the bullet hit him in the neck, and he passed away there."

Surinderpal is the general secretary of the large Gurdwara (Sikh place of worship and community) on East Park Road. He has lived in the area since he came to England in 1963. His grandfather's brother fought for the British Indian Army during the First World War. He was killed in Africa.

"His name was Jagat Singh. He was in the First World War and other people from his regiment, and also another person from the same village we came from, was with him... They ran out of ammunition in his

The Wider World

bunker and there was some ammunition laying nearby. He went to pick this ammunition container up, and his comrade said 'No, I will do it' and pulled him back. But he insisted and lifted his head up, and the bullet hit him in the neck and he passed away there."

Jagat Singh is 'Remembered with Honour' on the Dar Es Salaam British and Indian memorial in East Africa. His grandfather was married at the time, and Surinderpal has only recently discovered that his widow

"was married off to his younger brother....This was the normal tradition in those days, especially if one brother passed away and there was one that was not married. She would marry him."

Even though she remarried, his grandmother received a pension

"until her late 80s, when she passed away...which was very unusual. You didn't usually get a pension in India... It depends on where you came from in India and what connections you had. I think because there was more than one from the same village, there was a delegation to see the people you had to see about a pension, and so they got their pension."

Surinderpal's grandfather was recruited into the civil service as a "patvari" who measures land and places markers to indicate who owns it. He thinks he was given this position because his brother had fought in the War, and that his own service would also have helped secure the pension. The family lived in a very low-lying village called Moranwali. They had been living in Khuroopur near Jalandur

"but had been ousted from there because the British wanted to build barracks,"

which are apparently still there today. The whole village was moved to Moranwali, which previously had no houses and was just a swamp.

Surinderpal's father was only nine when his grandfather died. He came over to Britain in 1954 and lived in Highfields. His story at this point has some similarity to Pat's.

"There was a voucher system, as they were short of labour here...He settled in Leicester because he had an uncle here...105 St. Saviours Road, one of the most famous houses at that time...Most people who came over had to be in lodgings, and lots of people wouldn't have foreigners in their houses so they tended to congregate. Lots of people lived in the same house because they couldn't live anywhere else...such a

The Wider World

lot of discrimination...In this house, an Irish family and a Jamaican family and also 20-plus men - all men. The women came in 1963. We came in 1963 with my mum...Only a few families were there then ...They didn't buy any pots and pans 'cos they thought they would go back...just have the bare essentials to manage ... I remember going to 105 St. Saviours Road: always buzzing...It was quite an experience... big kitchen... communal cooking...Whoever was free, wasn't working, would do the cooking...until you got a job, you got free lodgings until you started earning and could pay something back."

Surinderpal Singh Rai

Today, the Gurdwara on East Park Road has a footfall of 20,000 people each week, most of whom are given food. Although mainly Sikhs, this number includes people from

"different communities coming in for the food, because of the austerity...This hospitality is part of our religion...We don't discriminate...We don't ask questions...We have rules about no drugs, and cover your head, and take off your shoes, but that's all...It is an open door policy."

Surinderpal's wife's grandfather was an official photographer for the British Indian Army. His name was Ganesa Singh, but Surinderpal hasn't been able to find any of his photographs.

▌ Kurdistan

Leicester is a so-called 'dispersal city' for asylum seekers. In 2014 there were 960 people waiting for a decision from the Home Office. In South Highfields there is housing for asylum seekers and the 'Open Hands' charity offers support, clothing and food to asylum seekers and others in need. Since 2000, hundreds of Kurdish asylum seekers and refugees have lived here. Their presence is more directly related to the First World War than any other group. It could be argued that they are here now as refugees because of what happened a hundred years ago.

The conflicts which have brought Kurdish people here from Iraq, Iran, Turkey and Syria are rooted in the actions of Britain and France during and after the First World War. Until the outbreak of the War, Kurdish people lived in the Ottoman Empire and Persia. The collapse of the Ottoman Empire gave Britain and France an opportunity to carve up the area to obtain access to the oil fields in the Middle East. Britain and France aimed to control the trade routes between Europe and Asia. Treaties signed between 1915 and 1923 did not take into consideration the needs of the people of the region. This left fertile ground for subsequent conflicts.

The Wider World

The Kurdish problem is a good example. As a result of the distribution of the Ottoman lands, Kurdish people found themselves placed in four different states: Iran, Syria, Iraq and the Turkish Republic. The interests of the Kurdish people were not taken into consideration and this led to the subsequent history of Kurdish struggle for either autonomy or independence in all four states. The asylum seekers who have been passing through Highfields make us question our role in the Middle East during the First World War, and the legitimacy of our involvement there in the 20th and 21st centuries.

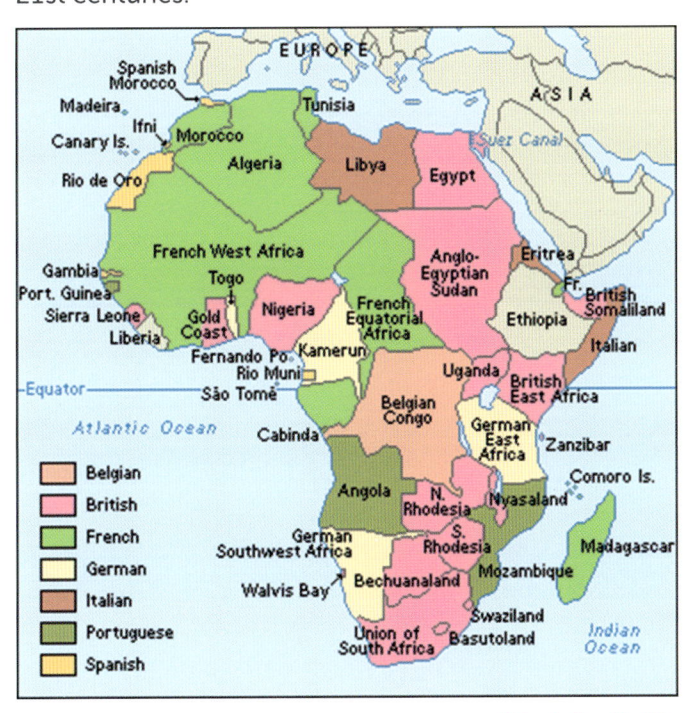

Africa before the War

▌Algeria

Britain was not the only European power with an Empire to expect colonised people to fight during the War. The French Foreign Legion had a long-established tradition of foreigners fighting for France. France also raised an "Army of Africa" largely made up of conscripts from Algeria, Tunisia and Morocco. These troops were called troupes coloniales. [98]

Mustapha Khodjet-Kesba

"They met their adversaries, the Germans, and they played football"

Mustapha is Algerian, and runs the Green Oasis Café on London Road. His grandfather fought in the First

75

The Wider World

World War. Mustapha used to spend time with him, and remembers his stories about the War and its impact on Algeria.

"I think he was in the War since it started. Many stories, especially in Verdun when he was in the trenches, fighting the Germans…some funny stories, jokes; they were trying to keep themselves amused. He was the grade of sergeant, with a group of Algerians. Not sure which platoon, but right at front. They gave them masks for the chemical gas. He saw many friends who died in front of him. They were giving him letters for their family before they went to the front for the assault. There's one thing which I remember very well. It was Christmas time. Muslims don't celebrate Christmas, but for them it was a kind of holiday, which is quite funny. They met their adversaries the Germans, and they played football which is quite unusual, but they celebrated all together. It was night time actually, and they greeted each other, and then the next day they started again, fighting each other. He was telling us how they met the Germans, and how they were talking … One of the Germans, he said to him 'Why are you fighting?' So my grandfather said to him 'For freedom'. So the German said to him 'No, we are fighting for our freedom!' My grandfather, he didn't understand what he meant by 'a German fighting for his freedom'."

As a country colonised by France, the Algerian people had little choice about fighting. Mustapha describes how it worked:

"The Algerians were taken by the French. Some of them were forced to go. Some enrolled in the army because they had nothing to do. Their families were starving; they joined the army to fight. Those that joined, they joined the Foreign Legion: La Légion Etrangère. It wasn't the case with my grandfather and many of the Algerians. They were taken, because, you know, they were considered as French subjects, to be taken to war. We were colonised by the French and we always looked at the French as the enemy. So it is hard to fight for someone who is mistreating you, like colonisers…in some ways it was … not a duty, but a kind of obligation, but they had to do it, they were forced, they did it."

Mustapha describes what it was like after the War:

"After the War people felt, actually they felt the tragedy of the War, not during the War, but after the War. Some of them were wounded; they had nightmares. My grandfather, I can't say he was psychologically affected. He was a very strong character. He was the kind of person, he was like a leader and had a very strong character. But he told us about the people he used to go and visit. Their lives were destroyed. You know, they had nightmares, some left their families, they were completely psychologically… it was a disorder in their life. And the wounded as well… they lost their arms, their legs, and the irony was… my grandfather said 'When we were going to war they gave us weapons and guns, but when we came back they gave us plastic arms, wooden legs and artificial hooks'."

"Marshal Petain, he visited Algeria to see the people who participated in the War. They were handing them crutches, things like that. It made their situation worse, because they couldn't support their families. There was no support, no pension."

Mustapha has his own childhood memory of injury:

"There was one person I remember. He had a black eye patch. And then one day, I asked my grandfather about it. I was kind of scared of him. His face was disfigured as well. I was about five years old, and when he used to come and see my grandfather I used to hide behind my grandfather. Some people used to come and ask my grandfather's advice because he was in the community, the kind of person people trusted, and they would ask him to solve their problems. Although he had a shop, he would sit outside when it was sunny and people would come and visit him. I would sit beside him in a

The Wider World

chair, and people would come. That man would come, and I used to hide, because he was quite scary. And he told me...not to be scared of him, because he lost his eye. He used to be a very handsome man. These were the tragic stories about people after the War."

Such was his grandfather's stature in the community, that he was chosen after the War to go on a delegation with Emir Khaled to the League of Nations to ask for basic rights such as owning land. His grandfather was not able to go, and Emir Khaled was not allowed to speak at the League of Nations as Algeria didn't officially exist. It was merely a province of France. However he did see President Wilson, who spoke on their behalf.

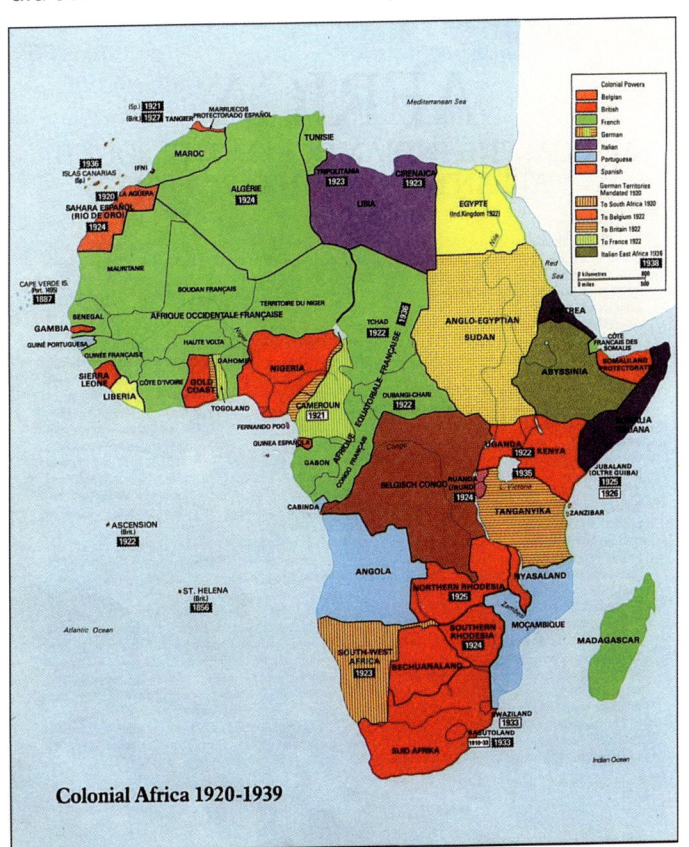

Colonial Africa 1920-1939

Africa after the War

The War changed political awareness and groups like 'The Star of North Africa' emerged, demanding independence. Momentum gathered, and on 8th May 1945 - VE Day - riots erupted between the Algerians and French settlers. Full independence came in 1962.

Mustapha, who was born in 1961, went to Paris in 1989 to study for a doctorate in molecular biology. In 1994 he came to London to take up a research post. He then moved to Cardiff and Edinburgh, where he met his Scottish wife. They eventually settled in Leicester in 2003.

▌Rwanda

In 1914 a debate took place among the colonial powers in Europe and Africa about the conduct of the War. Perhaps hostilities should be confined to Europe? War in the colonies could complicate matters. Telegrams were sent offering neutrality in Africa, but were overtaken by events on the ground. The first shots of World War One were fired on 6 August 1914, not in Europe but in the German colony of Togoland, as the French invaded from Dahomey (now Benin).

In Africa the European powers conscripted large numbers of civilians, not just as soldiers, but as 'porters', or rather forced labourers. More than two million men carried injured troops and supplies. About 400,000 died, mostly of disease or exhaustion.[99]

German troops in Cameroon, South West Africa (now Namibia) and Togoland soon surrendered, but the German garrison of German East Africa (modern-day Burundi, Rwanda and most of Tanzania) fought on until the end of the War. In 1916 a Belgian force invaded Rwanda and Burundi, and Belgium continued to govern them after the War.

Belgian rule, which continued until 1962, exploited the divisions between Hutu and Tutsi.

The Wider World

Eric Nkundumubano

"We've got this tension which is still there"

Eric comes from Rwanda and has been living in South Highfields since 2002. He does not have personal stories of the War, but is aware of its impact on Rwanda.

"Before the first World War, Rwanda was a German colony…. If you go to the east of Rwanda, at a place called Kibungo which is at the border with Tanzania, you can see some railway which the Germans had started because they had a project to connect all of Rwanda, and also to connect Rwanda with the rest of German East Africa. I think that included Burundi and Tanzania. When the First World War started that project stopped, and if you go to the border today you will see that there are railways which the Germans had started building because they wanted to expand… throughout German East Africa….We still don't have a railway system in Rwanda".

The train which never reached Rwanda going over a bridge on the River Ruvu in Tanganyika (Tropenmuseum Amsterdam)

Eric came to England as a refugee, following the genocide. It is open to debate how much the genocide was a result of the War and the takeover by Belgium.

Education was divisive:

"When the Belgians took over in 1919, the Tutsis, because they were in power, and the king was a Tutsi, they were favoured in terms of education. They had the privilege to go to the best schools. The only school in Rwanda was for the Tutsis. The only choice that the Hutus had was to attend missionary school, to become priests. It was attractive in the sense that there was education, everything was paid for, and there also there was the chance of travelling abroad to further your education. However, your destiny was to become a priest, and there was no running away from it. I would say the Tutsis had better education and choosing what they wanted to be. The Hutus, their choice was to study to become priests. The choice was limited for the Hutus."

To be a missionary you had to be Catholic.

"When the Belgians came after the First World War, there was this drive to discourage people from practising the traditional religion in Rwanda. The king was given a Christian name, and from thereon, that set the standard that all Rwandese had to adopt a traditional name and also a Christian name. This is something we see now…You will hardly see a Rwandese without a Christian name. …It was a difficult move because today in Rwanda the traditional religion or traditional beliefs are really practised in hiding, because in a way they are not seen as socially accepted. So it is accepted to be a Christian or a Muslim, but if you practise the traditional beliefs or traditional religion in Rwanda, it's a bit suspicious nowadays. So that was the consequence, of course, of the Belgians coming in."

The tensions between Tutsis and Hutus are still there:

"There is this feeling that the Hutus are now back in the Belgian colonial era, when the Tutsis were in power, with the king. The Hutus feel they should have a big say in who runs the country, because they are

The Wider World

the majority. The Tutsis, on the other hand, say 'For us to survive, we have to have a hand in running this country, because otherwise with the genocide....we can be easily exterminated.' I think there is a strong sense in the Tutsi community that they have to be in power for them to survive. So we've got this tension, which is still there. I think the Rwandese are very good at hiding their emotions. They don't talk a lot, and it's difficult at the moment, because people don't want to confront these issues. But I think the risk is these issues may explode one day."

Eric Nkundumubano (Photograph Dipak Mistry)

Eric describes his journey to the UK:

"I was born in 1980. I am a Rwandese citizen but I was born in Paris, and my father was a diplomat. After his mission we went back to Rwanda. I lived in Rwanda from 1983 until the genocide in 1994 when I was forced to go to Congo and seek asylum, and returned to Rwanda again in 1997 when war broke out in Congo. Then I had to flee Rwanda again in 2001, because again the situation was not good, and I and my family were in fear of our lives. I left Rwanda in 2001 and came to Britain and sought asylum."

When Eric was granted asylum he studied law at Leicester University. He has been working for the Red Cross Asylum Support Service since 2008.

▌ Trinidad and Tobago

Trinidad and Tobago were colonised for over five centuries by Spanish, French, Dutch, Courlander (from modern Latvia), and British colonists. Britain brought slaves from Africa to cultivate sugar, rum, cotton and indigo for export. The British banned the slave trade in 1807 and slaves were emancipated between 1834 and 1835. After this, indentured labourers were brought from India to meet the needs of plantation owners. During the War many Caribbean soldiers fought for Britain. These soldiers were often given dangerous, dirty jobs behind the line. Racist attitudes kept these soldiers segregated. [100]

Jean Hill

"The British West Indian Regiment...had to fight for their service medals"

Jean is from Trinidad. She has lived in Leicester since 1987 and taught at Medway School and Moat Community College. Her father fought in the Middle East during the First World War, with the British West Indian Regiment.

79

The Wider World

Jean Hill (photograph Dipak Mistry)

"He was a young man in his teens: seventeen. From my father's account, he joined the West Indian Regiment and left Trinidad for active service on the 27th March 1917 without being told where they were going. They left Trinidad via Grenada, Barbados, St. Lucia, Martinique, Gibraltar, Malta and then to Egypt in HMT Magdalena. They were escorted by a battle cruiser and then a British cruiser called 'The Berwick' from Malta, and then by two destroyers to Egypt, and were sent to the war front in August 1917.

He said they were sent within three miles of the enemy, guarding the generals whose objective was to take Beersheba, which was fought for and won about the 6th November 1917. He said the British also attacked Gaza....They lost men, and several wounded through bombing. Gaza was captured after five days of fighting and the British advanced to Jaffa and Tel Aviv a few weeks later. He said the day before Christmas 1917 the British took Jerusalem, and the West Indian Regiment were helpful in that victory by building a road, as the one road to Jerusalem was under constant bombardment. This was a place in the hills of Judaea, and after this victory they were sent to Lod to prepare to take part in the Jordan valley attacks.

When I was young he talked a lot about Australians.... and other soldiers he met from other parts of the Commonwealth... My father thought he was one of the fortunate ones who brought prisoners from the firing line, taking them to Jericho, not far from the Dead Sea. He believed that the British West Indian Regiment, the Australians, the New Zealanders, the Gurkhas, the Indians were the real heroes in that part of the world. One of the great things the British West Indian Regiment did was to capture a bridgehead over the Jordan river, which some Australians failed to do.

Personally, I don't think the British West Indian Regiment were treated as heroes after the War...I think they had to fight for their service medals, and I know that my father was reluctant to join up during the Second World War, although he remained staunchly British until his death at the age of 90. But I also think it gave him a different view of the British. Growing up in Trinidad in a colonial country, he looked up to them, but after the War he never quite did that again. He always spoke to them on the same level as he would speak to anybody else in this country."

Jean came over to Britain with her father on holiday when she was 16. Her mother had died the previous year.

"My father was to retire the year I was 16, and he was in the Trinidad civil service...They were given, on retirement, six months' holiday abroad, with their wives and two children."

The Wider World

Photograph of Jeans father in later life

Her father stayed on in Britain, but Jean went back to Trinidad. She returned to this country when she was 19. Her father tried to join the British Legion:

"He tried, and they wouldn't accept him. They didn't accept that he had been a soldier, and so he had to send off to the War Office for proof that he had been. But he still didn't bother joining...He didn't want to, after that."

Jean had enjoyed school in Trinidad.

"We had wonderful teachers. They were so dedicated to us... especially because it was a sort of growing nation, they wanted us to be interested in everything that was going on in the world. The English teachers as well, they really wanted us to succeed."

She went into teaching in Britain encouraged by her brother, who arrived here later.

"He pointed out to me that some children from a Caribbean background were being labelled as ESN in schools, and I couldn't really understand why, because most children that I knew in Trinidad, even if they didn't get into high school, knew all the rudiments. He was trying to get me to go into teaching, because he said... 'Jean, they're not dim, and I can't understand why they are being labelled.'"

At the time of the First World War in Trinidad, secondary education was only available to Christian children. This was difficult for the large Indian population, most of them Hindu, who had been brought over as indentured labourers in the mid-nineteenth century to replace the slave labour on the plantations.

"When my mother started high school, most of the schools in Trinidad, at that level, would have been Catholic or Anglican schools. The school my mother went to was founded by Canadian Scots and it was Presbyterian. It was a way of getting Indian children an education. If they became Presbyterian they would get an education in that sort of school. I've got a friend who would have been Sikh, because she's got Singh in her surname. I know her father became Catholic and they are Catholics, because she said it was the only way her father could get a job in the civil service in Trinidad. It wasn't just education, it was jobs, it was everything. So most Hindus and most Sikhs were forced to become self-employed. They opened shops; they became commercial people; they sold things door-to-door. Now, in Trinidad, they are quite well off. Our Prime Minister is of a Hindu background: the first woman Prime Minister. Before that, we've had one other Indian prime minister. Before that it was after independence, they were all from the black community. So that's changed, that's very good."

The Wider World

Countries	Total Mobilized	Killed & Died	Wounded	Prisoners & Missing	Total Casualties	Casualties % of Mobilized
Allied Powers						
Russia	12.000.000	1.700.000	4.950.000	2.500.000	9.150.000	76.3
France	8.410.000	1.357.800	4.266.000	537.000	6.160.800	76.3
British Empire	8.904.467	908.371	2.090.212	191.652	3.190.235	35.8
Italy	5.615.000	650.000	947.000	600.000	2.197.000	39.1
United States	4.355.000	126.000	234.300	4.500	364.800	8.2
Japan	800.000	300	907	3	1.210	0.2
Romania	750.000	335.706	120.000	80.000	535.706	71.4
Serbia	707.343	45.000	133.148	152.958	331.106	46.8
Belgium	267.000	13.716	44.686	34.659	93.061	34.9
Greece	230.000	5000	21.000	1000	17.000	11.7
Portugal	100.000	7.222	13.751	12.318	33.291	33.3
Montenegro	50.000	3000	10.000	7.000	20.000	40.0
Total	42.188.810	5.152.115	12.831.004	4.121.090	22.104.209	52.3
Central Powers						
Germany	11.000.000	1.773.700	4.216.058	1.152.800	7.142.558	64.9
Austria-Hungary	7.800.000	1.200.000	3.620.000	2.200.000	7.020.000	90.0
Turkey	2.850.000	325.000	400.000	250.000	975.000	34.2
Bulgaria	1.200.000	87.500	152.390	27.029	266.919	22.2
Total	22.850.000	3.386.200	8.388.448	3.629.829	15.404.477	67.4
Grand Total	65.038.810	8.538.315	21.219.452	7.750.919	37.508.686	57.6

World wide casualties

These stories in the second part of the book help us understand the impact of the First World War on people's lives around the world. They are intricately entwined with the Second World War and the history of their country, with changing borders, changing relationships with other countries and the changing nature of war. Chance so often played a huge part in their survival. We see this when Alice met the Woodcraft Folk in Czechoslovakia, and when the kind soldier in Kyrgyzstan lied to the authorities about knowing Jozef's father. By so generously sharing their journeys they have taught us about racism, about integration, about opportunity and how identity changes through the generations. For each of us, our place of birth is a matter of chance.

The First World War was the 'war to end all wars', yet even during the War itself that phrase was met with some scepticism. As Lloyd George put it: "This war, like the next war, is the war to end wars."

FINAL WORD

During the First World War South Highfields was a place of full employment. Its houses were 30 years old. People had moved here for work from other cities and also from other countries such as Germany and Russia, but most of the residents had been born in Leicester.

We have drawn on written accounts such as newspapers and council minutes, census returns and military papers, and on recorded interviews with people alive at the time. We have heard some remarkable stories - old and new. They have enabled us to create a picture of life in South Highfields during the First World War.

A hundred years later, unemployment is high in South Highfields. The houses are 130 years old and many have been converted to flats and hostels. There are now people living here from all over the world. This migration is partly a result of the First World War, which many argue led to the Second World War and continuing conflicts in places like Iraq.

Those of us involved in putting this book together have learnt a great deal from history and from those who are with us now. It has been a valuable experience. We hope you found it interesting too. We all carry the past with us.

FOOTNOTES

CHAPTER ONE

1. Ben Beazley, Leicester During the Great War p14
2. David Boulton, Objection Overruled p87
3. http://www.bbc.co.uk/guides/zcvdhyc
4. Matthew Richardson, Leicester and the Great War, p44
5. references for all the people interviewed and lodged at the East Midlands Oral History Archive are to be found at the end of these notes in alphabetical order of first name
6. Derek Seaton Sir Jonathan North: manufacturer, politician and philanthropist, Aspects of Leicester edited by John Hinks p67
7. Michael Howard the First World War A very Short Introduction p 46
8. St. Peter's was a church school and on Holy days in the year the children went from school to the church for a service
9. Records Office for Leicester, Leicestershire and Rutland (ROLLR) DE7243 Conscientious Objector's Autograph Book
10. Richardson p155
11. http://www2le.ac.uk/about/history-and-campus

CHAPTER TWO

12. 1911 Census
13. Ancestry : West Yorkshire Prison Records
14. 1902 Education Act full text http://www.educationengland.org.uk/documents/acts/1902-education-act.html
15. Leicester : Sanitation versus Vaccination by J.T. Biggs J.P. (1912) Chapter 30, Royal Commission Witnesses
16. England & Wales, National Probate Calendar (Index of Wills and Administrations), 1858-1966
17. http://www.nednewitt.com/whoswho/K-L.html
18. http://humanistheritage.org.uk/articles/sydney-gimsom
19. http://www.nednewitt.com/whoswho/G.html
20. Margot Cliff 1911 -1994 wrote her childhood memories which her daughter Gillian Lighton has kindly shared
21. 1911 census
22. Richardson p59
23. military-genealogy.com,comp. UK, Soldiers Died in the Great War 1914 -1919
24. British Army WW1 Service Records 1914 - 1920
25. Barnett.L.M. British Food Policy During the First World War (1985) p.4
26. Barnett p4
27. W.H.Beveridge, British Food Control (1928) p361
28. Lawrence Sondhaus, World War One:The Global Revolution (Cambridge :CUP, 2011),pp275-9
29. Richardson p41
30. http://www.womenslandarmy.co.uk/world-war-one/uniform/
31. Leicester did not become a City until 1919
32. Beazley p139
33. Twentieth report to the City Council 1st April 1912 to 31st March 1924 from City of Leicester Museum and Art Gallery
34. http://www.parliament.uk/about/living-heritage/transformingsociety/livinglearning/school/overview/1914-39
35. school log book ROLLR DE3063_2_Medway_St_Logbook_1903_38
36. 2013 price calculated per http://www.measuringworth.com/ukcompare/relativevalue.php.
37. Beazley p 162
38. http://www.craxford-family.co.uk/getperson.php?personID=I9559&tree=Craxford1
39. thanks to Friends of Welford Road Cemetery and Leicester, Leicestershire and Rutland Family History Society for allowing access to their database
40. Museum report to City Council as in note 32
41. Eileen Buchanan. Dr Charles Killick Millard and Public Health 1901-1934 Aspects of Leicester p148
42. Buchanan p150
43. Sue.Macrell Early Days April 2014 p12
44. Beazley p37
45. Beazley p38
46. Macrell
47. Cynthia Brown, 'Respectability and economy:death and funeral customs in Leicester in the Earlier Twentieth Century'.Aspects of Leicester pp163-4

CHAPTER THREE

48. Panikos Panayi, The Enemy in our midst: Germans in Britain during the First World War (New York:Berg, 1991) pp1, 27, 48, 50-51, 94
49. Panikos Panayi, The Enemy in our midst: Prisoners of Britain:German civilians and combatant internees during the First World War (Manchester: Manchester University Press, 2012)

FOOTNOTES

50 Panikos Panayi, The Internment of Aliens in Twentieth Century Britain, Immigrants and Minorities ed Cesarani and Kushner 1992

51 Because any German men between 17 and 45 were technically considered liable for military service, they were classified as 'reservists' by the British Government, and therefore a threat.

52 F.P.Armitage, Leicester 1914-18: the War Time Story of a Midland Town (Leicester;Backus,193x),p295

53 Leicester Chronicle and Leicester Daily Mercury (15th August 1914)

54 Panayi, Prisoners in Britain, p42,47

55 LDM (2nd February 1917)

56 1911 Census

57 1891 Census

58 LDM (2nd February 1917)

59 Willibald Richter, Hints for the Systematic Study of Finger Exercises on the Pianoforte, with special regard to the needs of Beginners (Liverpool: The Music Publishing Co-operative Society)

60 LDM (1st February 1917)

61 NA HO 144/3116/9. The bundle HO 144/3116 contains the various papers dealing with Richter's application for naturalisation, internment, denaturalisation and permission to return, however many are missing.

62 Translation in NA HO 144/3116/2

63 LDM 1st February 1917

64 NA HO 144/3116/2

65 NA HO 144/3116/16

66 NA HO 144/3116/16

67 NA HO 144/3116/16

68 NA HO 144/3116/21

69 NA HO 144/3116/23

70 NA Ho 144/3116/31

71 NA HO 144/3116/30

72 HO 144/3116/42,/45

73 HO 144/3116/52

74 http://www.historylearningsite.co.uk/lusitania.htm

75 Lawrence Sondhaus, World War One:The Global Revolution (Cambridge:CUP,2100), pp.276, 307

76 Panikos Panayi, 'Anti-German riots in London during the First World War', German History, 7, 2 (1989), 184-203

77 LC and LDM (15th May 1915)

78 M.Richardson, p27

79 http://www.historylearningsite.co.uk/lusitania.htm

80 Paniya, Enemy in our Midst pp 53-4, 187

81 Panikos Paniya, German immigrants in Britain during the nineteenth century, 1815-1914 (Oxford, 1995) p 202

82 LDM (8th January 1918)

83 LDM (8th January 1918)

84 LDM 15th January 1918)

85 LDM (14th January 1918)

86 LC (5th January 1918)

87 LDM (31st July 1918)

88 Armitage, p294

89 LDM 2/1/1918

90 Minutes of Proceedings of the Council from 9th November, 1918, to 28th October, 1919 (Leicester: Leicester City Council, 1919) 25/2/1919. pp78-9

91 Minutes of Proceedings of the Council from 9th November 1917 to 5th November 1918 (Leicester:Leicester City Council 1918) 1/1/1918, pp42-3: 30/7/1918, pp178- 80; 29/10/1918, p218. Minutes Highways and Sewerage Committee Minutes November 1914 - April 1919, 13/7/1917, p330; 12/10/1917, p 339; 30/11/1917, p353; 10/5/1918, pp400-401; pp7/6/1918, p406; 21/6/1918. p412; 18/10/1918, p435; 14/2/1919, p479

CHAPTER FOUR

92 Sondhaus, World War One, pp.16, 185

93 Sondhaus, p.337-9

94 Tackling Selective Mutism, A guide for professionals and Parents, edited by Benita Rae Smith and Alice Sluckin, Jessica Kinsley publishers 2014

95 Sondhaus, p.343.

CHAPTER FIVE

96 http://www.bl.uk/world-war-one/articles/colonial-troops

97 Howard, pp.50-51;Sondhaus, p.27

98 Sondhaus, p.27

99 Adam Hochschild, To End All Wars p349

100 William Kelleher Storey, The First World War (Plymouth, 2009), p.61.

APPENDIX

Those from South Highfields known to be in the military in WW1 according to available records.

STREET	SURNAME	FIRST NAMES	REGIMENT	ENLISTED	DISCHARGE KIA/DOW COUNTRY
Avon Street 25	Smith	Fred Sandal	Leicestershire Yeomanry	underage at enlistment 1915 Oct	1915 Nov
Avon Street 44	Fower	Ernest	Royal Army Medical Corps	1915 Dec	1919 Aug
Avon Street 50	Garner	Joseph	Royal Engineers, 129th Field Coy	1915 Apr	1916
Avon Street 55	Allen	Edgar Cecil	Durham Light Infantry	1917 Jan	1919 Mar
Bartholomew Street 16	Dawson	Edgar Charles	3rd Reserve Regiment of Cavalry: Royal Fusiliers, 2nd Bn: Royal West Kents	1917 Apr	1919
Bartholomew Street 27	Cooke	Harold	Army Service Corps, 1 Aldershot Coy conscientious objector	1916 Apr	?
Bartholomew Street 49	Eales	George Percy	Royal Garrison Artillery, 180 Heavy Battery, 46 & 185 Siege Battery	1915 Dec	1919 May
Bartholomew Street 59	Cox	Arthur Edwin	Royal Engineers, Railway Construction Company	1915 Dec	1919 Jul
Biddulph Street 20	Mounteney	Frank	Leicestershire Regiment	1915 Jun	?
Biddulph Street 23	Wrighton	Frances	Leicestershire Regiment, 53rd YS Bn: Royal Army Service Corps, No 1 Coy.	1918 Aug	1920 Jan
Biddulph Street 24	Sheasby	William Thomas	Army Service Corps, 53rd Remount Sq	1915 Oct	1918 Oct
Biddulph Street 33	Ironmonger	Edward Partridge	Royal Engineers	1915 Dec	1919 Feb
Biddulph Street 72	Jackson	Leonard	Army Service Corps, Mechanical Transport	1916 Jun	1919 Dec
Biddulph Street 90	Miller	William	Royal Engineers	1915 Apr	1918 Dec
Biddulph Street 111	Phillips	Thomas John	Machine Gun Corps, Heavy Section: Tank Corps	1916 Feb	1919 Feb
Brookhouse Avenue 11	Bryant	Albert Henry Curtis	Royal Garrison Artillery, 268 Siege Battery	1915 Nov	1919 Mar
Brookhouse Avenue 25	Israel	Morris	Royal Engineers, Railway Troop #brother-in-law	1915 Aug	1919 Jul
Brookhouse Avenue 25	Reynolds	James Edwin	Royal Field Artillery, 176th (Leicester) Bde & 235th Bde -#brother-in-law	1915 Jun	1920 Mar
Cedar Road 14	Easingwood	Percy	Leicestershire Regiment: South Staffordshire Reg, 5th & 6th Bns	1915 Dec	1918 Sep
Cedar Road 32	Bourne	Frank	Leicestershire Regiment: South Staffordshire Reg, 10th, 4th, 7th & 3rd Bns	1916 Feb	1919 Jan
Churchill Street 8	Bonsor	Frederick William	Hampshire Regiment, 4th Reserve: Lincolnshire Regiment, 4th Bn	1917 Apr	1919 Mar
Churchill Street 32	Gee	George Edgar	Royal Garrison Artillery, 23rd, 80th & 59th AA sections	1915 Dec	1920 Jan
Churchill Street 34	Allen	John Tom	Royal Field Artillery, 176th (Leicester) Bde & 160th Bde	1915 Jun	1920 Jun
College Avenue 5	Collins	Harry	Army Service Corps, 53rd Remount Sq	1915 Sep	1919 Feb
College Avenue 18	Barker	Albert Roper	Royal Engineers	1899 Oct	1920 Oct
College Avenue 26	Phipps	Ernest Albert	Rifle Brigade, 7th Bn ?	1917 Sep	Belgium
College Street 3	Hubbard	Reginald Ernest	Royal Field Artillery, 176 Bde	1915 Aug	1915
College Street 25	Newstead	John Howard	Royal Garrison Artillery, 145 Siege Battery	1915 Dec	1919 Jan
Conduit Street 47	Goode	Douglas Berthall	Army Cyclist Corps	1915 Dec	1919 Oct
Connaught Street 2	Capel	George	Leicestershire Regiment 4th Bn: Royal Scots 2/4th Bn	1915 Mar	1917 Jun
Evington Road 15	Nichols	Lionel Walter	Royal Sussex Regiment, 3/6th Cyclists Bn & 2nd Bn	1915 Dec	1917 Jul Belgium
Evington Road 35	Catlow	Harry Faulkner	Royal Fusiliers, 31st & 10th Bns: Army Service Corps 309 Coy	1915 Dec	1919 Sep
Evington Road 36a	Collins	Sidney William	Non-Combatant Corps: Army Reserve W conscientious objector	1916 May	?
Evington Road 61	Mansfield	Horace William	Leicestershire Regiment, 1/4th Bn	1914 Sep 1	915 Oct France
Evington Road 68	France	George William	Royal Field Artillery, 176th (Leicester) Bde, 34th Trench Mortar Battery	1915 Jun	1920 Mar
Evington Road 119	Dixon	Frank Shaw	Leicestershire Regiment, 4th Bn: Royal Engineers, 2/1st N Midland Signal Coy	1914 Sep	1919 Feb
Evington Road 157	Gaunt	Albert	Royal Flying Corps: Tank Corps	1915 Dec	1919 Jan

APPENDIX

STREET	SURNAME	FIRST NAMES	REGIMENT	ENLISTED	DISCHARGE KIA/DOW COUNTRY
Evington Street 33	Dove	Maurice Neville	Leicestershire Regiment: 16th Rajputs (Lucknow Regiment)	1916	?
Evington Street 33	Dove	Joshua	8th Labour Battalion, 1001 (Russia) Labour Company	Enlisted as an alien 1918 Apr	?
Glebe Street 4a	Boyles	Arthur Herbert	Royal Garrison Artillery, 434 & 13 Siege Battery	1915 Dec	1919 Mar
Glebe Street 4a	Brain	Edward	Royal Engineers, Chatham Depot & HQ Gen Staff 5th Army	1915 Dec	1919 Feb
Glebe Street 7	Brown	William Henry	Army Service Corps, C Coy & 24 L/C Supply Coy	1916 Mar	1920 Mar
Gordon Avenue 11	Brown	Samuel	Royal Garrison Artillery, 83 Coy	1915 Dec	1919 Jun
Guilford Street 13	Smith	Reuben	Royal Garrison Artillery, 342 Siege Battery	1915 Dec	1919 Feb
Hanover Street 7	Daffern	Cyril John	Leicestershire Regiment, 11th Bn: South Staffs Regt 3rd & 6th Bn	POW 1917 Feb	1919 Mar
Highfield Street 11	Snow	Albert	Leicestershire Regiment: Lancashire Fusiliers, 3/5th & 2/8th Bns	1916 May	1919 Nov
Highfield Street 40	Turnbull	Reginald Ernest	Leicestershire Regiment, 2/5th	1915 Dec	1917 Sep 4th CCS
Laurel Road 21	Bates	George Edgar	Durham Light Infantry, 6th Bn, 5th (Reserve) Bn	1915 Dec	1919 Dec
Laurel Road 23	Willson	Benjamin	Royal Garrison Artillery, 160 & 117 Heavy Battery: Royal Engineers	1915 Dec	1918 Apr 5th CCS
Laurel Road 31	Beese	John Mathew	Royal Navy	1907 Oct	1946 May
Laurel Road 35	Roberts	Albert Ernest	Durham Light Infantry, Labour Corps	1916 Jan	1919 Mar
Laurel Road 49, Highfields Hotel	Garner	Frank Percy Warner	Royal Engineers	1916 Jan	1919 Feb
Laurel Road 60	Venables	Leonard	Coldstream Guards, 3rd Bn	Previously served in Egypt 1906	1918 Apr Belgium
Laurel Road 62	German	George Donald	Royal Army Medical Corps	1915 Sep	1919 Feb
Laurel Road 72	Sarson	Reggie	Leicestershire Regiment: Lincolnshire Regiment, 12th Bn: RAMC	1916 Jul	1919 Sep
Laurel Road 93	Laundon	Percy Charles	London Regiment, 15th (Co. of London) Bn: Army Service Corps	1915 Dec	1919 Sep
Lincoln Street 12	Gabel	Cyril Solomon	Army Service Corps, Mechanical Transport	1917 Feb	1919 Oct
London Road 25	Craig	Robert Walker	Army Ordnance Corps	re-enlisted with temp commission upon discharge 1916 Mar	1917 Jun
London Road 31	Bollard	John	Royal Army Medical Corps, 2nd Nth Midland Field Ambulance	1914 Sep	1919 Feb
London Road 93	Margolies	Ivor	Sherwood Foresters, 18th Bn: Yorkshire Regt, 13th Bn	re-enlist temp comm 1915 Dec	1917 May
London Road 104	Millet	Isaac Moses	Middlesex Regiment, 30th Bn	?	1918 Jan
London Road 111	Wright	Henry James	Honourable Artillery Company, 1st Bn	1915 Jun	1919 Mar
London Road 139	Gibbs	Charles Henry	Army Service Corps, Mechanical Transport	1915 Oct	1918 Apr
London Road 165	Smith	Frederick Elliot	Royal Army Medical Corps, N.Mid Fd.Amb	re-enlisted with temp commission 1915 Nov	1916 May
Lonsdale Street 9	Harvey	Frederick Charles	Army Service Corps: Machine Gun Corps, 49th Bn	1915 Sep	?
Mecklenburg Street 10	Gimson	Joseph Yeomans	Royal Flying Corps: Tank Corps, 16th Bn	1915 Nov	1919 Mar
Mecklenburg Street 22	Weatherhead	Leslie Dixon	Indian Army: Army Chaplains Department, Devonshire Regiment	1917	1919
Medway Street 35	Rowe	Ernest	Royal Garrison Artillery, 9 Siege Battery	1915 Dec	1919 Mar
Medway Street 67	Slater	Henry	Durham Light Infantry, 2/8th Bn, 5th Res Bn & 9th Bn	1916 Feb	1919 Feb
Melbourne Road 24	Brown	George Henry	Leicestershire Regiment, 11th & 9th Bns	1915 Nov	1918 Apr ?
Melbourne Road 71	Bloxsom	Charles	Sherwood Foresters, 19th Bn: Durham Light Infantry, Labour Corps	1916 Apr	1919 Apr
Melbourne Road 71	Bloxsom	William Henry	Sherwood Foresters, 19th Bn: DLI Labour Corps – younger brother to above	1916 Apr	1919 Sep
Melbourne Street 7	Chew	James	Durham Light Infantry; Army Service Corps, Mechanical Transport	1915 Dec	1919 Jul
Mill Hill Lane 14	Gadsby	William Henry	Army Service Corps, Mechanical Transport	1915 Oct	1918 Oct

APPENDIX

STREET	SURNAME	FIRST NAMES	REGIMENT	ENLISTED	DISCHARGE KIA/DOW COUNTRY
Mill Hill Lane 20	Reeve	George William	Army Service Corps	1916 Jan	1919 Jul
Myrtle Road 69	Farmer	Harold	Army Service Corps, Mechanical Transport: Cheshire Regt	1914 Aug	1919 Feb
Myrtle Road 71	Clarke	George Hignell	Royal Engineers, Road & Quarry Troops – awarded Military Medal	1915 Dec	1919 Jan
Prebend Street, Studley House	Wright	Walter	Machine Gun Corps, 57th Bn & 171st Bn	1915 Dec	1919 Feb
Roslyn Street 36	Cooper	Charles William	Royal Army Medical Corps, 2nd Training Bn	1916 May	1918 May
Roslyn Street 7	Ancott	Alfred	Royal Garrison Artillery, 392 Siege Battery, 8th & 11th Mountain Bde	1916 May	1920 Feb
Saxe Coburg Street 1	Bryan	Clement Arthur Douglas	Royal Army Medical Corps	Known to be serving in Oct 1918	
Saxe Coburg Street 22	Klee	John Ceslau George	Leicestershire Regiment, 4th Bn: Middlesex Regiment, 30th Bn	1914 Aug	1917 Sep
Saxe Coburg Street 22	Klee	Aloysius Dominic	Middlesex Regiment, 30th Bn – younger brother to above	1916 Jun	1919 Jan
Saxe Coburg Street 27	Edgar	Arthur	Army Service Corps	1915 Dec	1919 Feb
Saxe Coburg Street 27	Webb	Athelstan Sylvester Kenshole	Northumberland Fusiliers, 7th Bn		1918 Mar France
Saxe Coburg Street 31	Widdowson	William Peacock	Royal Engineers, Special Brigade	1917 Mar	1919 Jun
Saxe Coburg Street 35	Stork	Bernard	Leicestershire Regiment, 1/4th Bn	1915 Oct	France
Saxe Coburg Street 54	Keene	Arnold Victor	Royal Fusiliers, 7th Bn – younger brother to next		1918 Apr France
Saxe Coburg Street 54	Keene	Charles Robert	Royal Army Medical Corps	1914 ?	
Skipworth Street 54	Hopcroft	Horace Philemon	Royal Horse Artillery (Leicestershire)	1911 Sep	1915 Mar UK – died after op. for appendicitis
Skipworth Street 81	Gill	George Harold	Royal Field Artillery, 35th DAC & 50th Bde	1915 Dec	1920 Feb
Skipworth Street 89	Jeffries	Arthur James	1st Bedford & Herts, Labour Corps	1917 Feb	1919 Oct
Sparkenhoe Street 2a	Bushrod	Reginald John	Sherwood Foresters: Durham Light Infantry, 25th Bn	1916 Feb	1918 Jun
Sparkenhoe Street 7	Bowley	William Cheshire	Regt, 7th Bn: 7th Labour Corps	1915 Aug	1919 Mar
Sparkenhoe Street 8	Hopkins	Percy Thomas	Northamptonshire Regt, 3rd & 7th Bns	1915 Nov	1917 Nov
Sparkenhoe Street 18	Pulford	George Ernest	Royal Engineers	1915 Dec	1917 Nov
Sparkenhoe Street 25	Crow	George Frederick	Labour Corps	1917 Aug	1918 Jan
Sparkenhoe Street 28	Kemp	Joseph Howard	Royal Engineers 4/1st N.Mid.Division	1915 Sep	1916 Jul
Sparkenhoe Street 29	Benn	Wilfred Edwin Herbert	Army Service Corps	1915 Feb	1919 Apr
Sparkenhoe Street 56	Cooper	William	Army Service Corps, Mechanical Transport 339,282,335,363,594, 717,593 Coy	1915 Apr	1919 Feb
Sparkenhoe Street 63	Coltman	Eric	Leicestershire Regiment, 4th Res Bn	1914 Sep	1915 Nov
Sparkenhoe Street 66	Wattam	Thomas William	Army Service Corps, TF	1914 Sep	?
St Albans Road 10	Beckett	Ernest Whitton	Leicestershire Regiment, 1/4th Bn	1918 Mar	France
St Albans Road 33	Gilbert	Guy	Royal Garrison Artillery, 147 (Leicester) Heavy Artillery	1915 Oct	1918 Aug
St Peters Road 13	Copson	Cyril Edgar	Army Service Corps, 246 & 924 Coy, 12 Cavalry Brigade Field Ambulance	1916 Aug	1920 Feb
St Peters Road 46a	Eaton	Fred	Machine Gun Corps, 213th Bn & 62nd Bns	1915 Nov	1919 Mar
St Peters Road 51	Taylor	Walter	Royal Marine Artillery, Howitzer Brigade	1916 Aug	1917 Nov Belgium
St Peters Road 53	Inglesant	John Herbert	Leicestershire Regiment, 4th & 10th Bns	1914 Aug	1916 Sep ?
St Peters Road 54	Gaskin	Charles Henry	Royal Army Medical Corps, 2nd London Sanitary Company	1918 Jul	1919 Feb
St Peters Road 66	Cholerton	Arthur Edward	Army Service Corps, Mechanical Transport 259, 562 & 611 Coys	1915 Feb	1919 Jun
Sutherland Street 9	Green	James William	Non-Combatant Corps, 3 Northern Coy - conscientious objector	1916 May	?
Sutherland Street 27	Barker	Samuel Harry	Leicestershire Regiment, 4th Bn: Lincolnshire Regiment, 13th Bn	1914 Nov	1917 Feb
Sutherland Street 29	Moulden	Harry	Royal Defence Corps, 159 & 160 Coys – old soldier age 51 yrs	1916 Sep	1919 Apr
Tichborne Street 5	Cooper	Harry Osborne	Army Service Corps, Mechanical Transport	1915 Dec	1919 Mar
Tichborne Street 10	Beeby	John	Main Royal Garrison Artillery, 2/2 London, 181 & 15 Heavy Battery	1916 Nov	1919 Dec

APPENDIX

STREET	SURNAME	FIRST NAMES	REGIMENT	ENLISTED	DISCHARGE KIA/DOW COUNTRY
Tichborne Street 35	Wacks	Joseph Braham	Leicestershire Regiment, 6th & 1st Bns	1915 Apr	?
Tichborne Street 59	Clarke	George	Royal Army Medical Corps, 2nd N.Mid.Fd.Amb	1915 Sep	1919 Feb
Welland Street 2	Bull	Horace Ewart	Leicestershire Regiment, 8th Bn	1914 Sep	1915 Feb
Welland Street 12	Murdock	Sidney George	Royal Field Artillery: Tank Corps, 15 Bn	1915 Nov	1919 Mar
Welland Street 21	Wright	Horace John	Royal Irish Regiment, 3rd, 7th & 5th Bns	1917 May	1919 Apr
Welland Street 30	Lilburn	Arthur Edward	Royal Garrison Artillery, 198 Siege Battery	1915 Nov	1919 Feb
Woodbine Avenue 14	Merry	Fred	Grenadier Guards, 7th, 3rd, 4th & 1st Bns	1915 Dec	1920 Mar
Woodbine Avenue 20	Nette	Herbert Henry	Royal Garrison Artillery, 254 & 223 Siege Battery	1916 Jun	1919 Apr
Woodbine Avenue 23	Halewood	Adam	Royal Garrison Artillery, 196 Siege Battery	1915 Dec	1919 Jul
Woodbine Avenue 25	Chapman	Tom	Army Service Corps, Mechanical Transport	1915 Apr	1919 Mar
Woodbine Avenue 26	Wells	Ernest Samuel	Royal Army Medical Corps	1916 Jun	1917 Nov
Woodbine Avenue 29	Woodward	Cyril Gordon	Army Service Corps, Mechanical Transport	1915 May	1916 Jan
Woodbine Avenue 36	Isaac	Thomas	South Wales Borderers, 2nd Bn	?	1915 Aug – killed in the Gallipoli campaign

EAST MIDLANDS ORAL HISTORY ARCHIVE REFERENCE NUMBERS

Historic recordings in alphabetical order of first name

Anne Martin 0994 LO/349/300
Betty Kendall 1026 LO/381/332
Doris Langham 006, MA200/006/006
Ellen Norris 800, LO/164/115
Herbert Orton 1050, LO/397/348
Hilda Stacy 1181, LO/528/478
James Allcock 1027, LO/362/333
Joe Wardle 1040, LO/395/346
Joseph Brown 1141, LO/488/438
Lawrence Woodward 1061, LO/408/359
Lillian Smith 870, LO/234/185
Mrs. Marston 720, LO/088/039
Sidney Coleman 0695 LO/062/013

Recent interviews in alphabetical order of first name

Alexander Kazmierz 2431, SS/01
Alice Klaus 2432, SS/02
Angela Walker 2433, SS/03
Eric Nkundumubano 2434, SS/04
Felicity Kuhivchak 2435, SS/05
Ilija Preocanin 2436, SS/06
Jean Hill 2437, SS/07
Jozef Jundzill 2438, SS/08
Mehmet Aydin 2439. SS/09
Mustapha Khodjet-Kesba 2440, SS/10
Patrick Breen 2441, SS/11
Piotr Kuhivchak 2442, SS/12
Surinderpal Singh Rai 2443, SS/13

REFERENCES FOR IMAGES FROM THE RECORD OFFICE OF LEICESTER, LEICESTERSHIRE AND RUTLAND

Chapter One

p8   DE3736_1158
p10 DE3736_1186
p11 DE3736_ 1195
p12 DE7243 Conscientious Objector's Autograph Book
p14 DE3736_1082

Chapter Two

p15 DE3736_Saxby_St_Box 27_postcard
p18 DE3736_Mecklenberg_St_box 22
p20 DE3736_Wellington_St_1914
p22 DE3736_ 1174
p23 DE3736_ 1212
p26 DE3736_Waterloo_St_1918
p27 DE3736_ 1179
p28 DE3736_ 1183
p32 DE3063_2_Medway_St_logbook_1903_38_p181 and p182

Chapter Three

p40 DE3736_1202
p44 DE3736_1216
p45 DE3736_ 1191
p45 DE3736_ 1126
p45 DE3736_1197
p47 DE3736_Mecklenberg_St_Box 22